**MARY JANE WALKER**

**Mary Jane Walker** is a writer of historically well-informed travel memoirs that come with an autobiographical flavour.

Travelling around the USA by train was an adventure in itself. Mary Jane met people from all walks of life and shades of opinion. Not only was she confronted by politics in the height of the 2016 election season, but also discovered environmental and conservation issues.

Mary Jane took Amtrak trains to Glacier, Grand Teton, Rocky Mountain and Yosemite national parks before the snow hit. She loved the Smithsonian Museums and after seeing a live dance at the Museum of the American Indian in Washington D.C., she decided to go to Standing Rock. It was a protest over land rights and drinking water, at 27 °C below zero!

Mary Jane was awed by a Detroit which is reverting to a park, by Galveston and by Birmingham, Alabama. She was tired of being mistaken for being a homeless person because she had a backpack, and left San Francisco because of it.

**Email: maryjanewalker@a-maverick.com**

**Facebook:** www.facebook.com/amavericktraveller

**Instagram:** @a_maverick_traveller

**Linkedin:** Mary Jane Walker

**Pinterest:** amavericktraveller

**TikTok:** @amavericktraveller1

**Twitter:** @Maventicktravel0

# a-maverick.com

MARY JANE WALKER

Published 2021 by Mary Jane Walker

A Maverick Traveller Ltd

PO BOX 44 146, Point Chevalier, Auckland 1246

NEW ZEALAND

**a-maverick.com**

ISBN-13:

978-0-473-58932-5 (softcover POD)

978-0-473-58934-9 (mobi)

978-0-473-58933-2 (epub)

978-0-473-58935-6 (digital audiobook).

**Disclaimer**

This book is a travel memoir, not an outdoors guide. Although the author and publisher have made every effort to ensure that the information in this book was correct at the time of publication, the author and publisher do not assume and hereby disclaim any liability to any party for any loss, damage, or disruption caused by errors or omissions, whether such errors or omissions result from negligence, accident, or any other cause. Some names have also been changed to disguise and protect certain individuals.

**Notes on Images**

All maps and aerial and satellite images have north at the top unless otherwise stated. All photographs in the book are the property of Mary Jane Walker unless otherwise credited.

**Covers and Fonts**

The front cover shows an artistically redrawn map of AMTRAK passenger services. The rear cover includes a composite year-2012 public domain image of the contiguous 48 states of the USA, courtesy NASA Earth Observatory/NOAA NGDC, which is blended into the artwork. Front cover and spine fonts are Impact Condensed. The interior text is typeset primarily in Garamond except for the image captions, which are Times New Roman.

# *Contents*

# A Note on Maps and Images

If you have a copy of this book in which the images are printed in black and white, or if you have a reader with a black-and-white screen, you can see all of the images in this book that were originally in colour in full colour, and all of the images including chapter-specific maps generally at higher resolution, by going to the blog posts linked at the end of each chapter.

In fact, these blog posts will generally contain more images and other visual material than appears in the book.

Unless noted or indicated otherwise, all maps, aerial photos and satellite images are shown with north at the top.

Readers are in every case urged to make use of original maps (often zoomable if online) and guides when in the outdoors; the maps and aerial/satellite images shown in this book are purely for illustration.

For a literally more all-round perspective, you might also wish to look at some of localities I describe in the 3D view on Google Earth.

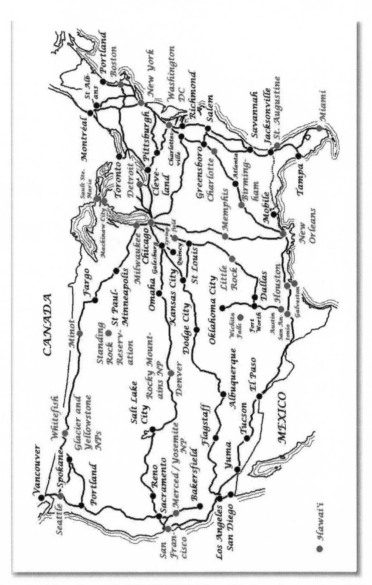

*Places that Mary Jane visited in 2016/2017 (in red in the colour version of this image), superimposed on a map of Amtrak passenger rail lines.* Rail services shown as a dotted line east of New Orleans were closed down after Hurricane Katrina in 2005 but are now being restored. Amtrak Thruway bus lines are not included in this map.

# Introduction

EVER since my first visit, I have been fascinated by American society. Everywhere I have gone in the United States, the richness and diversity of the cultures in in that county has always amazed me. The USA has also gone through periods of domestic polarization: the Civil War, the Great Depression, the McCarthy Era and the Vietnam War.

Little were we to know how this would erupt during the Trump years!

The country really is a melting pot of peoples and pouring out of the pot are completely new and organic cultures.

People also say that the USA is the Rome of the modern world. Though if that is the case, I think that there are also some parallels to the decline and fall of the ancient empire these days, the country obviously in some degree of decay amid a general dumbing down of culture and knowledge, and with the fundamentalist Christians a bit like the Taliban as well.

It seems extraordinary to me in recent months that Covid was allowed to hit so many communities hard, even well-organised cities like New York, which also saw its subway underwater during Hurricane Sandy, a foreshadowing of the climate change that might make much of the country unlivable if it continues. The attempted coup in January 2021 and the near attempt on Mike Pence's life saw a democracy turn in on itself. From my place in New Zealand this was like a nightmare.

Hopefully things won't quite get to the same point as in ancient Rome, but you never know.

*'Destruction' by Thomas Cole (1836), part of a series called 'The Course of Empire', public domain artwork reproduction via Wikimedia Commons. Image significantly brightened for reproduction.*

I left for the United States a month before the elections of 2016 and visited again in 2018.

In 2016, I wanted to get a first- hand impression of what the US society was like under President Barack Obama, before his second term was out. The degree of inequality for such a nation struck me as very surprising, with minimum wages lower than in many other countries including New Zealand.

I made my way around the lower forty-eight states and Hawai'i (I'm saving Alaska for another time), riding the rails with an Amtrak train pass, hiring fourteen rental cars, and taking a domestic flight at one point when ground-level travel got to be too much. I almost circled the lower forty- eight twice. Hours and hours and miles and miles of American soil racked up under my feet.

Riding on the train meant that I met still more people from all walks of life and political persuasions.

For the first two months, I spent a lot of time in and around the so-called 'Bible Belt'. In that part of the country most of the people I met seemed to be voting for Donald Trump over Hillary Clinton.

If Putin did put Trump in, it is understandable that the Russians might have wanted to interfere after the damage done in Afghanistan, Syria and the CIA attack on Russia in Chechyna, And, to think that the Chinese vaccine has been supplied to most South American countries and not the US-made vaccines – how this mighty power has fallen.

Under Joe Biden, little has changed amongst US foreign policy. Just a gentler domestic policy towards the vaccine and economic recovery.

This does not mean that America fell in love with Donald Trump. There is a lot of truth to the argument that he did not win the election, but rather, that Hillary Clinton lost it.

Moving on from politics, the outdoors was another major reason I wanted to visit the United States. I managed to get to several of the major national parks such as Grand Teton, Yosemite, Colorado National Park, and others, before winter arrived in earnest.

The national parks are one of the most impressive things about the United States. When I was writing my book *A Maverick New Zealand Way,* which talks about the national parks in my home country, I discovered that the United States was the first country to initiate the idea of a national park. In 1872, the US Congress and President Ulysses S. Grant created the world's first national park, Yellowstone, which is in the three states of Montana, Wyoming and Idaho.

I hired a total of fourteen rental cars and stayed in cheap hotels. I have some tips for travelling in Chapter Three, including apps.

I met so many people who had encountered grizzly bears and mountain lions; and they used bear-proof containers for their food. I had even seen people go as far as to set up portable electric fences around their campsites. Everyone was carrying bear spray. This was all very new to me.

I also got to visit and revisit cities and towns around the USA. In these urban areas, homelessness now seemed to be a major issue. I didn't see it so much the first time I visited the United States, some time before.

. An airport bag with rollers on it isn't practical on a road trip, let alone in the outdoors, so a backpack is my preferred form of luggage. I ran into other travellers who were encountering the same issues (perhaps this is the difference between a tourist and a traveller: a tourist has an airport bag, a traveller a backpack!).

When I went to the 50th US State, Hawai'i, I went camping. I was surprised that all the campsites and most of the beaches closed at 9 p.m., and I soon figured out why: namely, homeless people. I met a lot of homeless people, and talked to them and, really, it is just down to bad luck. It could have been anyone.

There was a time there were I was meeting homeless people for three to four days straight, I was amazed by their stories; they were all very sad. The local people in Hawai'i believed that their state was a dumping ground for the mainland's homeless, who came to Hawai'i for the abundance of wild fruit and vegetables and for the mildness of the winter.

Having introduced myself and my travels, I now turn to Chapter One.

CHAPTER ONE

# On the Amtrak Tracks

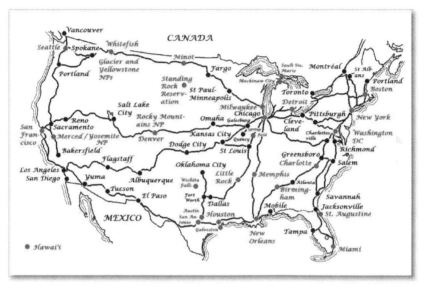

*Places that I visited in 2016/2017 (in red in the colour version of this image), superimposed on a map of Amtrak passenger rail lines.*

Rail services shown as a dotted line east of New Orleans were closed down after Hurricane Katrina in 2005 but are now being restored. Amtrak Thruway bus lines are not included in this map.

I GOT the idea of riding the Amtrak tracks after watching a TV series called *Billy Connolly's Tracks across America,* in which the Scottish comedian Billy Connolly went all round the USA by train.

'That looks like fun!', I thought. I loved how he got to meet the people: he was greeted in Montana by country music as he got off the train and met a woman with over 100 pieces of Elvis Presley memorabilia, things like mirrors and key rings! It sounded so interesting and down to earth, and if I did the same thing, I would be able to sit back and enjoy the scenery as well.

For me driving in the US was hard to get used to because it's the opposite side of the road to New Zealand, and we sure don't have Interstate Highways like they do in the US! Although having said that, the Interstates are probably safer than New Zealand's winding roads.

It made total sense to take the train. And so, when I was in Texas, I bought an Amtrak pass costing $900 for a 45-day, 18-segment journey, valid for the more than 500 destinations that Amtrak stop at, in 46 out of the 48 contiguous states of the USA. Amtrak trains don't visit Wyoming or South Dakota, nor Hawai'i nor Alaska. Otherwise, you can get to every state and to Vancouver, Toronto and Montréal in Canada as well, though you have to pay a bit extra when running on Canadian track as the Amtrak pass is strictly for US use.

(All prices given in this book are in US dollars, by the way!)

The pass isn't the same thing as a ticket. You use it to get the individual tickets for what Amtrak call segments, each segment a single journey in which you get on the train and get off or, if no train goes where you are going, an Amtrak Thruway bus. These often run between rail tracks in sections of America where the tracks don't meet. The pass is valid for getting a ticket on most of these, also counting as a segment.

The price of the pass covers sit-up seating in Coach Class. On some trains, it is possible to upgrade a segment to Business Class or a sleeper. The latter is recommended if you are planning to sleep on the train, as you probably won't be able to sleep otherwise. The most affordable sleeper accommodation for one or two people is what Amtrak calls a Roomette, which seats two across from one another and converts to bunks.

You can check out all these options on Amtrak's website, namely, amtrak.com.

I did a heap of research on the American rail system. Rail travel is on the rise across the US because it is cheap, and also, because it is becoming fashionable again in the face of crowded airports and obtrusive airport security checks, which are putting people off flying in a big way. A further advantage of trains is that the main stations are in the middle of cities whereas airports aren't. And wi-fi and other electronic technologies have also revolutionized the potential productivity of time spent on the train.

The glamour has gone off cars and air travel alike these days. Who would have thought the old technology of the train would come back into vogue?

As the city centres have once more become fashionable and gentrified, this has added to the appeal of the train. All that America needs now are genuinely high-speed trains of the sort they have in Europe and Asia. Outside of the Northeast Corridor, the almost continuously urbanised area between Boston and Washington D.C. that is served by the up to 150 mph (240 km/h) Acela Express. The Acela is Amtrak's most glamorous service and the only one with First Class seats in addition to Business Class (there are no Coach Class seats on Acela).

Apart from that, Amtrak services are slow and sedate, considering the distances that are involved. Train speed limits in the USA are mostly 79 mph (126 km/h), a speed limit that dates back to 1947, and American trains often don't make that speed.

The (relatively) slow speed of most American passenger train services remains a handicap, though it is fair to say that many people ride the rails precisely to get away from a world where everything is in a rush.

Amtrak is a passenger-only service, run by the US Government. It was founded in 1971, when the US Government took over 336 passenger rail routes that had become unprofitable and pruned them back to 184. The Amtrak trains often have to give way to freight trains, and this is another reason why Amtrak services are generally slow.

The exception that proves this rule is the Acela high-speed service between the major cities of the north-eastern seaboard, which reaches 150 mph in places (240 km/h), though only in places as even the Acela has to give way to freight here and there.

*Joe Biden and Senator Arlen Specter on the Acela with members of the Middle Class Task Force on 27 February 2009, US Government Public Domain image via Wikimedia Commons.*

Joe Biden, who actually has something of the common touch and more genuinely so than Trump, used to ride the Acela and other Amtrak trains to and from Washington when he was Vice-President just like any other commuter, to the point of acquiring the nickname 'Amtrak Joe'.

As Biden got to be more famous his tickets were booked under other names to foil would-be assassins, though apart from that he still kept commuting on the train just like anybody else even when Vice-President, racking up an estimated 8,200 round-trip commutes to the consternation of his bodyguards. Biden regrets that now that he is actually President, it really does now have to be all helicopters and stuff and the old informal days are over.

The hand-me-down nature of Amtrak stands in sharp contrast to the spread of high-speed rail in China, which has expanded from nothing in 2007 to 38,000 km (24,000 miles) of track by the end of 2020, with roughly as much again expected to have been built by 2035.

If America were China, most of the Amtrak tracks I travelled on would be high speed rail routes, and probably all of them by now. That is another reason to suspect that America has seen better days.

Instead, the Americans seem to attribute a sort of museum-like significance to their railways, with rich people, firms and celebrities trundling about in private carriages, known as 'private varnish' because they tend to have a lot of old-fashioned wood panelling.

So, I might have spotted someone famous on one of my train journeys! And a journey some of the rides are. It's easy to rack up hours and hours on the trains getting from A to B. My first Amtrak segment, a six-hour journey from Houston to New Orleans, was really nothing but a scratch on the surface of America.

*Private varnish carriages at Denver Union Station. Photo by Kenneth C. Zirkel, 30 December 2015, CC BY-SA 4.0 via Wikimedia Commons.*

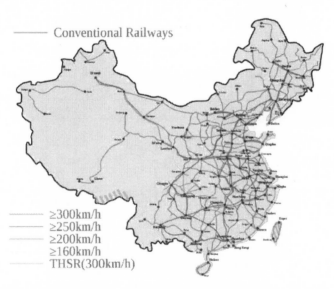

*High speed rail tracks in China as of 2020 by Ythlev, 2 January 2020, CC BY-SA 4.0 via Wikimedia Commons. Development of earlier work by Ibicdlcod. The image includes some conventional railways in grey and is most meaningful in full colour.*

Presumably, the longer the train takes to get to wherever it is going, the more the owners of private varnish get their money's worth.

Though it plays second fiddle to freight, Amtrak is subsidized so that people can get around cheaply and also, interestingly enough, in order to boost the viability of railways that might otherwise struggle if they were used only for freight.

My pass was strictly for long-distance cheap travel and did not extend to urban commuter trains, nor the Acela, nor to another popular service, the Autotrain, which runs between suburban Washington D.C. and a station near Orlando in Florida.

The Autotrain enables people from the cold north-east to travel to and from Florida with their cars, while at the same time avoiding an unfeasibly epic drive through pretty much the whole of the Old South to get there.

People I met on the Amtrak trains said it was much cheaper than owning a car. Even so, Amtrak rail travel isn't just for poor people but for a mixture of people, cultures, occupations, education and ages. You had one lot of people who had low incomes, and then other people who paid $300 a night for a luxury sleeper, all on the train together.

For more, see:

**a-maverick.com/blog/on-the-amtrak-tracks**

CHAPTER TWO

# How the Land was Peopled

UNTIL the end of the last ice age, it seems that the Americas were unpeopled. But toward the end of the ice age, it became possible to walk across a land bridge from Siberia, a land bridge now called Beringia. Although the area was far north and fairly cold, it was free of ice because comparatively little snow fell in this region at the time. And so, the ancestors of the first native Americans were able to walk across, and then to walk south through other ice-free corridors in the western part of what is now Canada.

Thus were the Americas peopled for the first time. All native Americans, even those as far south as Patagonia or in the Amazon jungles, are related to people who still live in Siberia.

The first Europeans to find their way to the Americas, significantly so in view of the later European majorities in North and South America, were the Vikings: who did not, however, leave a lasting colonial impact. The Vikings island-hopped by way of Iceland and Greenland in the north, and the only parts of North American that they arrived in were fairly inhospitable.

Colonisation by Europeans began in earnest with the arrival of Christopher Columbus's fleet in 1492. Columbus himself became a colonial governor and was then removed from office for mistreating the indigenous inhabitants: a bad omen for the future.

Introduced diseases severely depopulated the continent, with an estimated native American population of more than twenty million in Mexico falling by ninety per cent in half a century, and seven hundred thousand in Florida dwindling to about two thousand by 1700.

An Aztec-like civilization called the 'Mississippian' culture covered much of the future United States but declined and fell due to disease with no European record of its existence, as European settlers hadn't got there yet, unlike the civilisations of Mexico which were recorded by the invading Spanish.

*'Three examples of Mississippian culture avian themed repoussé copper plates. The righthand figure is one of the Spiro plates from Spiro Mounds in Oklahoma. The left-hand figure is Wulfing plate A, one of Wulfing cache from Malden, Missouri. The middle plate is Rogan plate 1, from Etowah Mounds in Georgia. Examples of this type of artwork have been found as artifacts in many states throughout the Midwest and Southeast.' Photos by Herb Roe, chromesun.org, 2012, CC BY-SA 3.0 via Wikimedia Commons.*

It is something of a mystery as to why the original inhabitants of the Americas were so vulnerable to European diseases. The exact reasons continue to be debated. But the net result was that large numbers of European colonists were able to move in thereafter, under the impression that North America was an untamed virgin wilderness of forests, which had actually regrown on former farms and villages in many cases, inhabited by only a small number of native Americans.

There is even a theory that the regrowth of the forests sucked so much carbon dioxide out of the atmosphere that it contributed to the global cooling known as the :Little Ice Age, at its worst in the 1600s when the Thames river used to freeze over in London and when cold weather led to hunger and privation in the Old World, so that Europe itself was torn by wars to an even greater extent than usual.

*'Frost Fair' on the frozen River Thames near the Temple Stairs in the winter of 1683/84, public domain image by Thomas Wyke via Wikimedia Commons.*

The next thing to happen was the introduction of slavery, conventionally dated to 1619, though it began slowly and indeed, was not covered by any laws that declared anyone to be a slave at first. Among the American colonists the practice of slavery was not an age-old evil but one that they invented, or re-invented. Millions of slaves were eventually imported from Africa, and then bred locally, before being finally freed as a result of the 1861-65 American Civil War.

Although there is a myth that the black slaves were passively liberated by well-meaning whites in the Civil War, in fact about a quarter of the troops in the Northern, Union army were black or, as they were called at that time, U.S. Colored Troops.

*U.S. Colored Troops at a picket station (outpost) near the Dutch Gap Canal, Virginia. Photograph first published as one of a pair of stereo images in 1864. Public domain image via the Library of Congress.*

Immigration continued through the nineteenth and twentieth centuries, in ways that left distinct impressions on different parts of the USA insofar as birds of a feather tended to flock together. People from the same region of Europe, even the same village, would uproot themselves from the old country and come together once more at a chosen spot in America once more. Germans, in particular, were so numerous that it was thought at one time that the United States might become officially bilingual in English and German. Large parts of the country were certainly informally bilingual in English and German, known locally as Dutch, a corruption of *Deutsch.*

*Where historically recent immigrants have, typically, come from*

*Bilingual Flier in English and German, posted in Chicago in 1886.*
*Source: Library of Congress.*

And so, we move forward to the present day, in which there is a lively debate as to whether USA should have two official written languages or not, except that German has largely died out and the current debate is about whether Spanish should be the other language.

Today, there are great divides in America's society, some of them to do with ethnic groups and skin colour, but also to do with regional cultures and subcultures, of which some people, such as Colin

Woodard in his book *American Nations,* have counted as many as eleven. Much earlier, in his *Childhood and Society*, first published in 1950, the German psychologist Erik Erikson also described the USA as a land of polarities. Polarities such as:

Open roads of immigration and jealous islands of tradition; outgoing internationalism and defiant isolationism; boisterous competition and self-effacing cooperation. (1965 edn, p. 258)

The polarities today have included liberals versus the legacy of slavery and Jim Crow laws, scientists versus creationists, coastal areas versus the interior, and a tremendous residue of ignorance and prejudice and brutality in what is otherwise supposed to be a modern country. Thus, the USA remains notorious for its shootings, mass shootings and gun culture, problems that have actually got worse in the last few decades in some ways.

For more, see:

a-maverick.com/blog/how-the-land-was-peopled

CHAPTER THREE

# *Travel Tips*

HERE are some useful tips for the would-be traveller to the USA. First of all, American airports are often crowded, and it is no fun travelling during peak holiday seasons, including summertime and holiday weekends such as Spring Break.

The shoulder seasons, away from holiday weekends, are better.

As for getting into the United States, as a tourist-type traveller, what you do is apply for a Visa waiver online first of all, answer some questions, and obtain an Electronic System for Travel Authorization (ESTA) clearance, which only costs $14. If this does not work or if your country is not eligible, you have to apply for a visa, which generally involves an interview and costs more. Either way, your passport must be valid until six months after you plan to leave the USA.

You can use Travisa to organise a visa for you if you run into difficulties. Though of course you must pay for this service as well as for the visa. Travisa is also useful for other purposes as well, and worth checking out at least.

The Americans ask about earlier crimes and drug convictions, which can cause problems. Fortunately, in New Zealand we have a clean slate act which means that many past offences cannot be made public after seven years, and the act also applies to the filling in of foreign immigration questionnaires. You might have a similar law in your country.

I heard of a Kiwi visitor to the USA who had been arrested for drunk driving when he was nineteen. Even though he was now thirty-five and so didn't have to mention it under our clean slate act, he did anyway. With the result that he was detained for five hours at one of the American airports before they decided to let him into the country.

But that was nothing comparted to the misfortunes of another guy, who posted on social media that he was looking forward to taking part in a riot at a New York nightclub. Even though it was surely a joke, he was detained for no less than three days and then sent back to where he came from.

So, it is probably a good idea to make sure there is nothing like that in your social media posts or on your computer before you go. Nor, of course, to tell any sorts of jokes that might be misunderstood, even by somebody who is listening. They really are very security conscious.

**Travelling Around America**

As to travelling around, there are a lot of self-guided driving schemes that you can sign up for. However, I was travelling mainly by train, my car hire was just local. You can get lots of very cheap last-minute deals.

There are a great many car rental companies, including the home-grown Avis and Hertz groups and the French Europcar, as well as smaller independent operators.

When I arrived in Houston to do most of the travel described in this book, I had to fill in six pages of forms and get interviewed for an hour before they let me have an American SIM card for my phone.

The SIM only lasted six months, so when I came back to visit some people in Red Hook, New York, it had expired and I had to get a new one. I went into a phone shop in New York and said, I suppose I will have to fill in all that paperwork again. The shop staff seemed a bit nonplussed when I mentioned the word paperwork, so I explained how it had been in Texas, and they laughed and said that they do things differently down there! So, New York is a good place to get your SIM. They have fifty states, and each one has different regulations.

On the other hand, New York is a lot stricter about regulating Covid immunity. From 16 August 2021 onward, New York City has made it compulsory to show proof of Covid immunity in order to access restaurants, gyms and indoor entertainment, a set of places that will probably be broadened in the near future. As of the time of writing, enforcement was to start in September. There are two apps to choose from, the Excelsior Pass, which uses a QR code and stores some personal information, and is thus controversial, and the New York Covid Safe App, which simply stores images of WHO-approved vaccination cards, test results and so on. The Excelsior Pass is basically for New York State residents or those vaccinated in New York State, so tourists and visitors mostly need to use the New York Covid Safe App. At the opposite extreme, more than a dozen states have banned what they call such 'vaccine passports': these are generally the states where people don't wear masks so much, either (more on the mask wars, below).

Useful general apps for travellers, all of them with .com on the end, include:

**Airbnb,** for cheap places to stay and for events as well, which people tend to forget. In New York I went to jazz nights and rap nights, both based on info I came across on Airbnb!

**Booking,** for cheap hotels and other services.

**Groupon,** which is good for discount hairdressing services and eating out.

**HotelTonight,** for last minute hotel deals

**Meetup,** for hiking and other group activities such as cooking, eating out and even expat communities

**Travisa,** which I have already mentioned above.

**Travelocity,** for last minute hotel deals and other travel services. Not as focused on accommodation as HotelTonight.

**Tripadvisor,** which is very good for telling you what to do locally if you put your interests in.

As for the **Internet**, it is worth noting that public libraries seemed to offer free wifi everywhere I went.

For **national parks and the outdoors,** there are many government websites that tell you all about these places. I also found that **discovernw.org** was a great site about the northwestern corner of the lower 48 states of the USA.

When it comes to **medical matters,** you must have proper travel insurance, as medical care in the USA costs a fortune.

Apart from that, my loyal travel companion was my medical kit, which along with sticking plasters, bandages and scissors contained the diarrhoea stopper loperamide, some ciprofloxacin antibiotics, packets of Gastrolyte rehydration solution and Tramadol, Tiger Balm, Vaseline for dry skin, tea tree oil, iodine and bandages, and, finally, plain old paracetamol. Not exactly a romantic set-up, but realistic, nonetheless.

And also, be up to date with **vaccinations** before you go, **insurance** of every kind, and **travel advisories.**

Starting overleaf, here is a list of things that I find it useful to pack for outdoors trips.

GEAR

- Backpack (about 70 litres capacity)
- Plastic liner (essential)
- Travel towel (small)
- Raincoat
- Over-pants (preferably waterproof)
- Warm hat
- Gloves
- Sun hat
- Shorts
- Hand gel
- Lip balm
- Survival bag
- Sunblock
- Insect repellent
- Crocs or light hut shoes
- Torch (preferably a head torch)
- Long johns, x2
- Woollen socks (one pair per day)
- Boots
- Sleeping bag
- Wool singlet, x2
- Wool t-shirt, x2
- Long sleeve wool top, x1 or 2
- Fleece top, x2
- Underwear

- Sunglasses
- Camera
- Stove
- Cooking gas
- 1.25L water
- First-aid kit including blister Band-Aids
- Lighter & waterproof matches
- Food*
- Billy, mug, bowl, spoon and sharp knife
- Snap-lock bags for food
- Plastic bags to divide clothes etc.
- Toilet paper
- Toiletries, small and light
- Dishwashing liquid & a small pot scrubber
- Pack cover (useful if it rains)
- Compass, survival kit& whistle
- Map
- Puttees or gaiters (optional)
- Strips of rubber
- Rope
- Pocket knife
- Orthotics/soles/Vaseline/wool to wrap around toes
- Thin cloths cut in two, for washing self and dishes
- Waistband with pockets
- Cheap reading glasses
- Candle

FOOD SUGGESTIONS

- Scroggin (mixed nuts & dried fruit)
- Dried meals (I like Kathmandu, a New Zealand brand)
- Couscous
- Camembert & Cheddar cheese
- Marmite/jam/chutney in film containers
- Hot chocolate/cappuccino sachets
- Tea bags
- Muesli/porridge
- Instant custard mix
- Mashed potato (dried)
- Soup mix
- Dried vegetables
- Cuisine rice
- Crackers/pita breads
- Dates and dried apple, mango& apricots
- Milk powder
- Gluten-free falafel mix (with rice and Thai chilli sauce!)
- Packet of sweet-and-sour sauce mix and pine nuts
- Eggs
- Miso soups and instant packet soups
- Hard boiled eggs
- Energy drinks, eg. Hairy Lemon sachets
- Packet biscuits – don't bother about pudding
- Marshmallows

*Lastly, a few other tips:*

Always carry a spare mobile phone with international SIM in case yours gets lost with its US SIM. Also carry spare sunglasses and light.

You may also wish to hire a personal locator beacon. And always advise rangers of travels and discuss wildlife, diseases and hazards.

A bear fence to place around your tent may be needed in some places, along with bear spray.

Carrying butane for stoves, matches and lighter will probably not be possible on the plane.

And of course, in the present Covid crisis, you should watch out for anti-maskers. In the words of Umair Haque, from a Medium.com column called 'Covid is Now Officially Going Permanent' (August 20, 2021):

Ultra conservatives don't "believe in" masks and vaccines. I put it in quotes because facts exist whether or not you believe in them. And yet one thing that America's Red States and the Taliban have in common is that they don't want people to get vaccines or to wear masks, unless you mean burqas. That's how regressive the American conservative mind is: on the issue of Covid, it's neatly aligned with…the Taliban.

As of the time of writing, the US Centers for Disease Control and Prevention have a webpage called the 'CDC Covid Data Tracker' that enables you to track Covid incidence state by state or county by county, and they also have a 'Covid-19 Travel Recommendations by Destination' page that provides similar information for international travellers.

For more, see:

a-maverick.com/blog/travel-tips-for-the-usa

CHAPTER FOUR

# Houston: my first landing

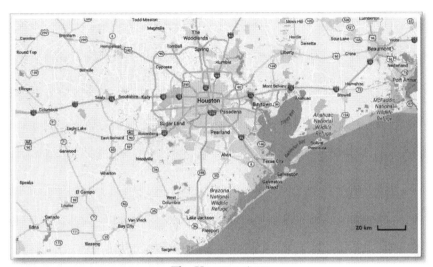

**The Houston Area**
*North at top. Map data ©2017 Google, INEGI.*

WHEN Neil Armstrong landed on the moon, the first word he said was "Houston".

I managed to grab a cheap flight from Auckland to Houston for less than $500. It was going to be the beginning of my travel around the United States, with the particular intention of witnessing the presidential election firsthand.

And what an election it would turn out to be: monumental.

I arrived at the George Bush Intercontinental Airport, or simply the Houston International Airport. With a population of over six million, the Houston metropolitan area is the second largest in Texas (just after Dallas- Fort Worth), and the fifth largest in the entire United States.

So, I arrived into American city culture at full throttle, engines pumping.

Houston sits on the banks of the Buffalo Bayou, a creek with several tributaries, draining a watershed of which Houston lies at the dead centre, and which meanders down into Trinity Bay, a sheltered inlet of the Gulf of Mexico.

Houston is one of America's fastest-growing cities. In 1900 the population of Houston was only about 45,000. The city really took off after nearby Galveston was devastated by a hurricane in that year: at which point it was realized that a more inland location, but not one so far inland that ships couldn't get to it entirely, would be a safer place to invest in the future. Houston, set a little back from Trinity Bay, fitted the bill; though it was itself prone to flooding, what with all those bayous meandering, in no hurry, through a flat landscape into an estuary that could itself be backed up with storm surges.

*Houston 3D Aerial View looking northward*
Imagery ©2017 Google. Map data ©2017 Google

The Hurricane Harvey floods, since I left, have been the worst to date; but there have been many devastating floods even before that.

In one 1930s flood, the downtown was under an incredible fifty feet of water, at least as measured above the normal creek level. It would be an exaggeration to say that Houston has been constructed in the middle of a Texas equivalent of the bed of Australia's Lake Eyre, but the region seems to have some similar characteristics.

In a heroic feat of public works, which had already been requested and approved before the Galveston Hurricane but was now treated with greater urgency, Trinity Bay and Buffalo Bayou, navigable for schooners, would be transformed into the modern Houston Ship Channel, navigable for large ships to within 13 kilometres of the very centre of Houston. A once-sleepy Houston never looked back after the Ship Channel was upgraded. Above the navigation limit, Buffalo Bayou was left in its natural condition, and these days it has esplanade parks and cycle tracks on both sides in the inner- city area.

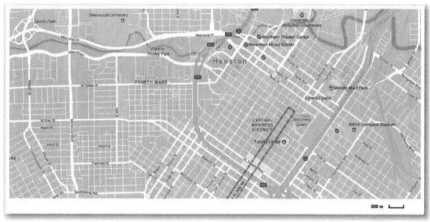

*Houston Downtown Map*
North at top. Map data ©2017 Google

The trams are very affordable: you can ride them all day for $3, or at least you could when I was there.

Filled with art museums, soaring skyscrapers and restaurants, the inner city of Houston was a place I really enjoyed visiting.

We tend to think of Texas as a land of hardy individualists. But the reality is that a city like Houston is quite well-planned; and, on top of that, owes much of its prosperity to government investments like the Ship Channel in addition to the various forms of private enterprise that came along later, after the government had literally cleared the way for it to proceed.

I got a taxi from the airport, using my Uber app. The taxi driver was from Pakistan, a lovely man who talked to me about the Urdu language of Pakistan and its differences from the Hindustani of India (mainly the alphabet, which in Pakistan is a Persian one that Iranians could read). He told me he had once worked for Homeland Security: which surprised me a little bit; and instantly brought back unwelcome memories of possible having been snooped on in Russia when I was there because of my Greenpeace connections. Anyhow, I was just here for the election and a good time.

I stayed in an Airbnb room for the first few nights in a district called Lawndale, about six kilometres southeast of downtown. The area was very multi-cultural and there were a lot of Latino and Mexican people living there. The room was run by a couple who I will call Janet and John.

Janet showed me to my room which was nice and clean, so I was thankful after the long flight.

I was surprised that most of the guests stayed in their rooms: they seemed to associate the outdoors with mosquitoes and bugs. They ran their air conditioning constantly, even though was the beginning of winter.

*Houston METRORail in downtown, 11 July 2006*
Photograph by 'eschipul', Wikimedia Commons, CC-BY-SA 2.0.

The very first night I arrived I was straight into it. I went to a Democratic fundraiser at a place called Art and Music. As a naïve outsider, I was surprised to find that most of the attendees spoke Spanish and were from Mexico or other Hispanic countries.

I met Kim Ogg, a woman running for district attorney in Harris County, which includes most of Houston, on a platform that included decriminalizing marijuana, and Ed González, a former police officer who was running for Sheriff.

The 2016 elections were not just for President of the United States but for a whole host of other offices as well, including legal and judicial ones such as district attorney and sheriff, or chief of police, which the United States is almost unique in putting up for election. The United States holds elections for a wide range of offices every two years, and every four years, they happen to include the President of the United States. The election for US President is much the only American election noticed by outsiders, but by no means the be-all and end-all of their democracy.

*My Airbnb Accommodation*

There were about twenty women there and we all had a laugh as we played a game called "Stump the Trump". As part of the fundraiser, they filled a piñata in the shape of Donald Trump with lollies and everyone had turn beating it with a stick for $20. The fundraiser was an excellent experience and I got to meet the Ms Ogg, Mr González, and a few other people who were running in the election. I texted my host family and asked did they want a Democratic sign outside their house, and they really took affront to that!

I had a few conversations with locals: things along the lines of the minimum wage, which was a shocking $7 an hour, although someone told me they were only paid $2.35! That made me feel bad and I made sure I tipped – which is something we don't do in New Zealand.

My first impression of Lawndale was that it was a really nice community, and Janet and John showed me around. I was driven around, and they pointed out housing developments to me, property developing was on the boom a bit here and they pointed out a house to me which had just been renovated and sold for $400,000. John took me for a drive to Bohemeos, a restaurant in the historical suburb of Eastwood. It was my kind of place, music, art and good coffee.

The woman who operated the shop played the guitar, and she had two sisters who were born in Mexico and lived in Texas. It was awesome sitting there and listening to the music from the guitar. I ended up walking back to my accommodation and it was a bit nerve-wracking because of all the dogs wandering around the streets. It probably wasn't the safest place to decide to go for a walk, after all.

I had to decide how I was going to get around Houston, Uber had been working fine but I had concerns in general about my safety travelling around especially on my own and at night. So, I did a few Google searches and found that Trip Advisor gave a few good suggestions.

I decided I would just relax, enjoy what Houston had on offer, get my act together and get my Amtrak railway pass. The pass was easy enough to get, although it was pricey $900. But that was an all-stop pass, so I could get on where I liked and get off where I liked. I thought I might look for other accommodation as well.

I ended up going to the Houston Art Fair, downtown. It was amazing and included art based on mugshots of famous people taken when they had been arrested (mostly because of protests I presume). My favourite was one of Jimi Hendrix; but then, I've got a painting of Jimi Hendrix on my own wall at home.

Texas seems to have a tradition of Mexican grills, lots of small restaurants with reasonably priced food, I went to the Lakeside Restaurant and that was nice.

*Houston downtown, above*

*The Lake House Restaurant, Discovery Green, top right*

*Bohemeos Café, right.*

The Art Gallery cost about $25 to enter but the art was fantastic. My favourite was rice-paper done in circles in different colours. I also saw some amazing sculpture art works by a couple of artists who grew up in Houston, Mark Flood and Will Boone.

Before I left, I was in the house talking to Janet about my wonderful day when John came in fuming. I got told off because I had left a door open on accident and let mosquitoes in. I couldn't relax when I got back there, the door wouldn't unlock, and I got locked in on my last day. What I did, was I got up early in the morning because I thought I had better get ready to leave. I had my SIM card, and the GPS was going fine.

So, I woke up early and got the car, and I hung around the Houston mall waiting for it to open. That was interesting – I ordered a large yoghurt – and it was so large it was like the size of a small container of popcorn like what you get at the movie theatres in New Zealand.

I had decided to visit Galveston and got a sudden urge along the way to make a detour to NASA's Space Center Houston. I soon realised it was one of the best impulses I'd had.

The Space Centre Houston is a space museum and education centre, close to the Johnson Space Centre which is where much of the more serious business of NASA is done. There is also another Space Center in Florida, the Kennedy Space Center.

The space center was well worth visiting, and it was interesting to learn about the visions they had of limitless solar energy on the Moon and industries that might one day be powered by it, including spaceships that might easily be launched from its feeble gravity by electric catapults called mass drivers, including satellites to capture even more solar energy in space and perhaps even beam it back to the Earth.

But all this is only feasible if there is water on the Moon, both to drink and to chemically convert into rocket fuel.

*Space Center Houston:*
*Photos include astronaut*
*Shower mannequin and*
*simulated flight*
*deck of shuttle*

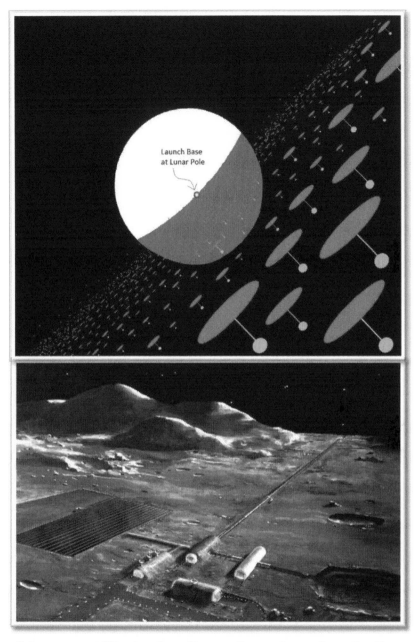

*Solar power satellites in polar orbit around moon (image drawn for this book) and impression of lunar mass driver, from 1977 NASA publication*
(Mass driver image Wikimedia commons, US Government public domain.)

The rocks that were brought back from the moon by the first astronauts proved that the Moon's craters were formed by meteorites and comets, rather than volcanoes. This made it likely that there was water, in the form of ice from comets, at the bottom of polar craters where the scorching rays of the sun could never reach.

All the same, ice was only proven to exist there much more recently. If it had been found back in the early 1970s, I think we would have kept on going back to the Moon.

Although NASA has achieved massive scientific discoveries with its unmanned space probes since 1972, I do still wonder whether the word 'Houston' may once more be spoken on the Moon, not too far hence. Perhaps it might.

For more, see:

a-maverick.com/blog/houston-my-first-landing

CHAPTER FIVE

# Galveston: I went there because of a song

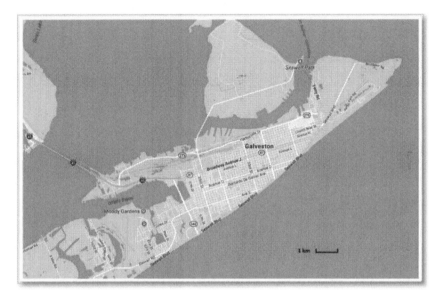

*Galveston*
North at top. Map data ©2017 Google, INEGI.

AFTER the Space Center, which lies just off the Gulf Freeway south- east of Houston, I carried on down to Galveston, which lies a few tens of kilometres south-east of Houston on a sand-bar bar island just off the coast. I found it hair-raising getting back onto the freeway the first time, since I was used to driving on the left and everybody seemed to be going fast in what was, to me, the wrong direction. Do you choose the right lane or the left lane? Quick, quick . . . best just get under the sign that says Galveston! I had wanted to go to Galveston because of the famous 1969 song by Glen Campbell, which my father used to listen to.

On the way into Galveston, I noticed some amazing residential housing areas, perched right by the water's edge.

On the side of the island that faced the rest of Texas, there was an oil port. There were tankers tied up, but nothing was moving, apparently because they weren't making enough from the oil to warrant drilling at that moment in time.

The residential neighbourhood near the port looked sparse and abandoned. I wondered whether a lot of the old houses had been blown down in the last big hurricane to hit the island, in 2008. Galveston is quite bit more gentrified and rebuilt on the other side, which faces the open sea and isn't so industrial; though the port district also has its run-down and seedy charms, including those of the nearby historic downtown area.

*Images of Galveston*

Stockpiled oil derricks, an old Coca-Cola sign, hurricane damage creating vacant lots, and the Flea on the Sea

Made from solid materials, the historic district mostly survived the great hurricane of 1900 which otherwise destroyed the town and killed thousands, because there were no proper warnings in those days. The fact that the island became a backwater thereafter means the historic district survives pretty much as it was in 1900, frozen in time like a fly in amber.

I walked around by the water. Galveston was an excellent place to walk around, with the same tight grid of square blocks as downtown Houston. At Pier 21, the touristy part of the port, I found that I could go on a dolphin cruise for $10. I asked around about that, and it pretty much everyone said that was the water was dirty, there were no dolphins and that was why it was so cheap!

I supposed the dolphins must have died or moved on because of the Deepwater Horizon oil rig blowout in 2010, which also put a crimp in the livelihoods of small fishers and boat operators in the area and was apparently still doing so.

I went and took the boat anyway and I met a young couple that had just got married in Dallas. It seemed to me that Galveston was a popular honeymoon spot for young couples from the mainland. Perhaps that's how Glen Campbell got the idea for the song.

We did see dolphins in the end, and we also saw some military bases on islands along the coast.

I went to a place called Flea by the Sea in the historic downtown area; an amazing bric-a-brac market, exactly the sort of place you'd expect to find in such a place.

I had lunch somewhere and the food was amazing, I had succulent prawns wrapped in crispy bacon. Absolutely yum. There were a lot of palm trees around Galveston which made it feel somewhat tropical. If it hadn't been for the cooler breeze, you might think you were on a Caribbean island.

Galveston is quite an old town. It is named after Bernardo de Gálvez, who at the time of the American Revolution was the governor of Louisiana, ruled in those days by Spain, which also controlled present-day Mexico and Texas.

In the end, I got in my rented car and drove back to Houston afterward (there is a causeway linking Galveston Island to the shore). I found it a worry driving, not just for the reasons I mentioned before, but also because there were so many one-way streets, and my GPS wasn't working because I had a New Zealand SIM in my phone. I almost turned right into two one-way lanes, got pulled up by the police, and I got a ticket and an official warning. I was pretty shaken by this stage and stopped for an almond cappuccino, which was really nice and setting, before driving on.

When I was on Galveston Island, I'd spoken to this guy who I thought was exaggerating about the risks of driving in the USA. I've since found out if you kill someone in a car you are liable to face more serious criminal charges than in New Zealand, so you have to be careful (as you should be, anyway).

So, I drove all the way back to Houston that evening feeling a bit ruffled. I had to drop the car back off at the Hilton before seven a.m. the next day, and I was over driving, so I dropped it off early and then had a beer at the Hilton before getting an Uber taxi to a new Airbnb place.

This Airbnb place was a worse disaster than the last one! After I left, the woman running it accused me of stealing a painting. She tried to claim $500 for the allegedly missing painting and said she was going to call the police, which sounded like a scam. It was so bizarre because

I had no use for a painting. How was I going to cart it all around the States with me? I was driving while at the same time of being accused of this. As she was texting me and threatening me, I decided I had better switch off the phone: but then my phone seemed to somehow stop working altogether. All this was stress I didn't need, that was for sure.

For more, see:

a-maverick.com/blog/galveston-i-went-there-because-of-a-song

CHAPTER SIX

# San Antonio: The Daughters of Texas, the Alamo, and Mexico

A FTER Houston, I drove to San Antonio along Interstate 10; nearly 300 km, with a stop-off in a little town called Harwood. Another thing I don't like about the US freeways is the amount of truck traffic. I was looking forward to getting on the railways. I should have got the Greyhound bus, because the day I drove to San Antonio was a day I really didn't need. San Antonio is an area of Texas rich in Spanish Colonial history and culture. San Antonio is the Spanish version of Saint Anthony. With a population of almost one and a half million, San Antonio is the second most populous city in Texas. It is not far behind the City of Houston, which has a population of over two million. The difference is that San Antonio is one city in political terms, whereas the City of Houston is part of a wider conurbation of six million.

San Antonio is surrounded by military bases and is also known for oil and gas industries. Tourism also accounts for a fair share of the local economy. There are some UNESCO World Heritage sites from the Spanish era, including the famous Texas Alamo.

Anyway, I drove to my Airbnb in Harwood, it was 8 o'clock and I waited for an hour and a half with my non-functioning phone. My Airbnb host had given me the street name of the property but not the number, and said she was waiting for me, but she wasn't. It was late at night, and I couldn't be bothered waiting around.

Before long it was 9.30 p.m. and I needed to find somewhere else to stay. I drove around looking for a hotel and found one: the owner looked me up and down and said it wasn't suitable for the likes of me. To judge by the characters that were staying there; this must have been intended as a compliment. So, I was glad to move on and try to find another place.

It was 11 o'clock at night before I finally found the Comfort Inn in Harwood. It was a nice place and I ended up staying for two nights. They had a swimming pool but as things turned out, I didn't have any time to enjoy it!

I went to one place that night and got a shrimp meal for about $8 but unbeknown to me, all the staff were only paid about $2 an hour. I found that out from a guy on the wait staff who said he made about $150 a day on tips, but that was working 12-hour days. He let his mother-in-law take care of the children, both because of these long hours and also to keep her occupied because she had lost her daughter, his sister-in-law, in a head-on collision (I wonder if one of the drivers was tired from long hours too?).

What tragedy all round. In Seattle, the current (2021) minimum wage ordinance specifies a pay rate of $13.25 per hour for small employers if the employees are earning $2 or more an hour in tips. That's not much, but better than the situation I've just described. They really do need to sort out a living wage in the US.

The Comfort Inn was run by a couple from Mumbai. The place was getting painted up and a lot of the people there were construction workers. All the white guys were voting for Trump, and they certainly didn't mix with the Spanish workers; that was interesting and frankly surprised me a bit.

The first day was hot, 90 degrees Fahrenheit with 80% humidity, and I headed into San Antonio to explore. San Antonio is amazing. They have redeveloped the inner city surrounding the San Antonio

River. On either side of the river there was an abundance of restaurants, hotels and gardens. It was really gorgeous. All along the river were remnants of Spanish occupation, with old historical buildings like schools and churches.

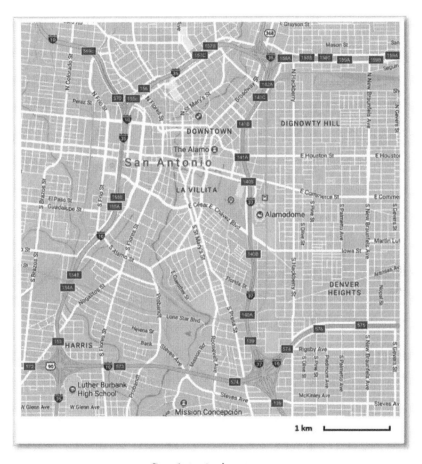

*San Antonio downtown*
North at top. Map data ©2017 Google

*San Antonio: The River Walk, and San Fernando Cathedral*

The food in San Antonio was great. I loved the steaks here and I saw lovely Mexican grills. I went into one restaurant to have an iced tea and this guy said to me that San Antonio was full of the underclass, drug addicts or whatever, they sleep on the side of the road and it's very sad. I was surprised at his remarks. He pretty much said San

Antonio is a place you just drive through because of the underclass. But whoever said that was wrong.

I saw one or two homeless people hanging out down by the river. I stopped in at a pizza joint to get an iced tea and I asked the guy behind the counter where was a good place to stay in the city. He bluntly said not too because of the homeless people, at night they wander around and play up. I thought that was quite critical and negative.

Wandering around San Antonio I didn't think it was all that bad, and I didn't mind it at all.

The Cathedral of San Fernando had operated as a church since the 1730s, though the current structure was more recent. I went to the Town Hall and saw some more buildings from the Spanish colonial era, which were pretty amazing.

San Antonio has good, cheap, public transport and doesn't sprawl unduly by American standards. It is more or less round in shape, with a well-defined downtown. An urbanized corridor extends all the way to Austin some 120 kilometres distant, and beyond, on the Interstate 35 freeway. San Antonio has a very extensive network of freeways including a complete ring around the historic downtown; fortunately, the historic downtown area is not too tightly squeezed between the freeways as the inner ring still encloses an area of about ten square kilometres or so.

I found a park in the downtown and decided to walk around and then I discovered I wasn't far from the site of the Battle of the Alamo, so I headed there which was really amazing!

The Alamo was originally built by the Spanish and was initially, and properly, known as the Mission San Antonio de Valero. Alamo, or Álamo more correctly, is a nickname meaning 'poplar' or 'cottonwood', a kind of tree in either case; and is thought to have come about because a company of locally recruited Spanish cavalry was stationed there in the early 1800s

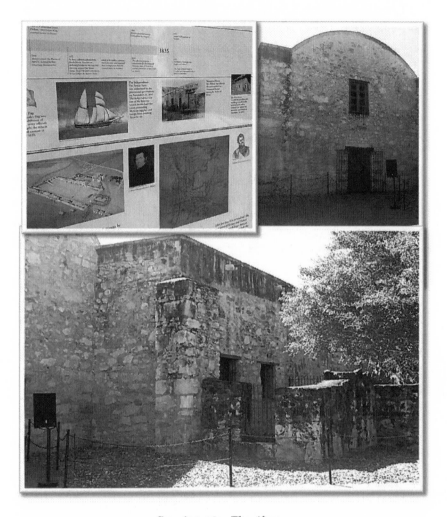

*San Antonio: The Alamo*

Sitting in the hotel restaurant the next morning, I got talking to a guy named Leonard over breakfast. He was homeless and he was applying for a job at a hotel and had an interview. We chatted over breakfast while he waited until it was time to be interviewed.

Leonard had been in a well-paid job with a house of his own before he became homeless but ended up with a boarder or flatmate who stole a lot from him. Then he ended up losing his job, and then his house, because of the recession and just never got ahead.

He was living in a night shelter in downtown Austin. He seemed very well spoken and presented and I didn't take him for having an addiction problem or anything like that: the usual, sad prejudgment we tend to have about homeless people.

I told him I'd take him out to lunch after his interview. We went to a Mexican grill, where we had steak, salads and a delicious taco dish. Leonard was really interesting, and I learned a lot from him. He was quarter Sioux and one quarter indigenous Alaskan, and his mother was in a rest home. He hadn't spoken to her in 10 years and his father died quite some time ago. Leonard said because of high property taxes and low income, his father had also lost the family home.

I asked him why he was still homeless, and he answered my question graciously. To rent an apartment in Austin is about $1000 a month, he said. I imagined that being single and on America's wretched minimum wages it would be hard to afford such a rate, though for a middle-class person it would have been a lot more affordable. Leonard was heading in the right track though, and he had got the job at the hotel: I was really happy for him. He said he knew a lot of the homeless people, but he wanted to stay away from them, which was understandable. It's easy to get the idea that bad luck is contagious.

Leonard told me how in Austin the homeless people were well looked after in comparison to other places. They got free health care and there was a state-run shelter. Then he had to get going so we said goodbye, and I went out and about in the city.

For more, see:

a-maverick.com/blog/san-antonio-the-daughters-of-texas-the-alamo-and-mexico

CHAPTER SEVEN

# *Austin: Free healthcare for the homeless, art and great music*

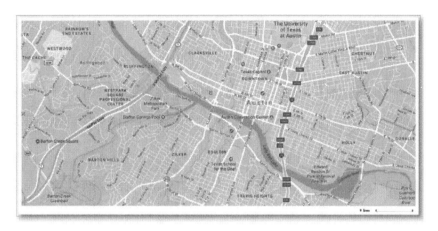

**Austin, downtown river precinct**
*North at top. Map data ©2017 Google*

AUSTIN is a sight for sore eyes, especially at night with the city buildings lit up in a rainbow of colours reflected in the cool waters of Texas's Colorado River. The latest census showed a little over 900,000 people lived within Austin City, and it is now the fastest growing city in the United States.

Austin was hit hard by the Great Depression of the 1930s and didn't really pick up until the 1980s. It is now home to offices of some big players in the technology field, firms like Apple, Amazon, Ebay, Google and IBM, so the city is thriving. I found it an interesting contrast even to San Antonio which is only an hour and a half away by car.

I met a number of homeless people, and I was warned to stay out of the downtown because of them all. As in San Antonio, the river area was beautiful, and I liked how they had modernised it all.

I went to the 7th District, and I parked the car for $15 for the whole day. I felt a bit tired and lazy and so I decided to jump on a Hop-On-Hop-Off Double Decker Bus Tour and go for a tour around the city.

There was plenty to see. We were taken past the Texas State Capitol building, past Lady Bird Lake, past a few historical museums, the Austin Convention centre and art galleries showcasing a range of cultural art exhibitions. There was a lot to see and do – that's for sure.

I heard that 65,000 people a year are moving to Austin, making it the fastest growing city in the entire USA. The Rainey district is still a lovely area to eat out (I have visited it before), and the 6th district is very vibrant with really good food as well. So, I walked around and ate lots of good food. I think Texas has some of the best food around, and it's all affordable and good value for money.

I spoke to a woman in an art gallery who said that Texas was still a very divided society, and that white people don't know a lot of people of colour. I was quite surprised when she told me that. She also told me how her family had pretty much abandoned her after she had married a man of colour. I thought back to that incident with the renovators.

I found plenty of differences between Austin and Houston. One thing I noticed, which sounds minor but is important, was that Austin had better pedestrian crossings than Houston: something that matters when you walk around a lot! They experiment with new ideas.

For instance, when I was there, one of the busiest intersections in Austin, at East 6th and Waller Streets, where the historic but deteriorating Uptown Sports Club is located, had its kerbs flared out on what looked like a trial basis with polka dots and edge marker posts to narrow the road carriageway and thus slow the traffic down. The polka dots, placed behind edge marker posts, served as a visual barrier. If it worked, presumably the intersection was then to have a permanent kerb buildout.

(Having said that, unfortunately, this trial seems to have faded away as of 2021. I hope something more permanent is about to be done.)

A woman on the bus tour told me that in the early 2000s, the Austin Independent Business Association had coined the term 'weird' to describe Austin. Austin seemed to be a pocket of Texas which was completely different to the usual cowboy stereotype, home to a much more urban vibe. I met another woman in an Austin movie house. She was born and bred in Texas, and she said Austin was like a bubble and it really is like an exception in Texas.

Perhaps some of this is down to the fact that Austin is the state capital and began its existence as a completely planned and brand-new capital in the days of the Republic of Texas: a bit like the later founding of Canberra in Australia. Austin has had a strong legacy of planning ever since those days, making it perhaps the most planned city in what is often otherwise stereotyped as a state of individualists. Having said that, there is plenty of evidence of civic pride elsewhere in Texas.

There was a three-day music festival on, with Kanye West and Willy Nelson; so, it was quite busy in the city. I did make a brief stop at number 6 Congress Street, which had some great live music.

Texas also has its Confederate legacy, and there was a statue there I found quite interesting, and I took some photos. Whether it'll still be there in the future is a good question.

*Austin*

The State Capitol with 'Six Flags' crests of Spain, France, Mexico, Texas Republic, Confederate States and USA.. Bottom row, from left: Cowboy statue by Constance Whitney Warren (1926), mounted Texas Ranger Statue, Confederate memorial.
State Capitol image Wikimedia Commons, photograph by Wing-Chi Poon, 15 December 2007, CC-BY-SA 3.0, architecturally rectified and slightly cropped for this book.

One other thing I did find remarkable is that there have been so many flags over Texas. There has been the Spanish flag, the French flag, the Mexican flag, the Texas Republic flag, the United States flag and the Confederate flag, as well as the Texas State flag.

It was interesting that they displayed and acknowledged various emblems of their history, though there were adverse comments from some of the locals I met.

As of the time of writing (2021), the Confederate Soldiers' Monument and Terry's Texas Rangers statue in the collage above are still present, as is the cowboy statue. So is the Confederate seal among the six seals.

Austin is home to the largest urban bat colony in North America. Over one million bats live under the Ann W. Richards Congress Avenue Bridge that was built over the Lady Bird Lake in 1910 and restructured in 1980 to support the increasing number of vehicles. The bat season attracts tourists who flock to the banks surrounding the bridge to see the Mexican free-tailed bats fly into the sky at dusk during the months of March to November usually.

The South Congress Bridge is open to the public to view the flight of the bats as they blacken in the sky with their sheer numbers. I made a point of stopping by the bridge to see them was great to see, black balls of fur and wings flit across the darkening horizon as the sun set. Apparently, they were once considered to be a big problem and the city actively tried to remove them, until an organization started up aimed at protecting them. They migrate every year to Mexico and as far south as Yucatan.

Austin in one day was not how I would have liked to do the trip; I really wish I had had more time. I had also decided I was going to use

Booking. com in these parts instead of Airbnb because I found I could get cheap hotels.

I also found the people in Austin were very friendly. I was filling up my car with gas, and someone came over and asked if they could check my tyre pressure for me and I said thank you!

You can go on tours of the stately homes in downtown Austin, in what is called the Bremond Block Historic District: it is definitely something to do if you have the time, either guided or just on your own with a map or an app.

Finally, it is interesting to note that Sam Houston, one of the early founders of Texas, had wanted the capital of the Republic of Texas to be the just-founded town that was also named after him: and so, there was a bit of a skirmish in 1842. In an incident called the Texas Archive War, Houston had ten men try to raid all the archives and take them to the State Archives to Houston.

This wasn't just a product of Houston's ego. At the time, there were renewed hostilities between Texas and Mexico, and the Mexicans reoccupied San Antonio. There was a good chance that nearby Austin, the brand- new capital of Texas, would fall next; and Houston was concerned that the archives would not survive.

Anyhow, Houston's party failed to get the archives shifted; Austin survived; and the Mexicans eventually withdrew back behind the Rio Grande. Houston became the capital of the Republic of Texas for the rest of its short history, but once Texas formally became a state in 1846, Austin became the capital of the state of Texas, and has been ever since.

It was time to get on the road again and I was off to visit my friend Aubray in Wichita Falls: a five-hour trip.

For more, see:

a-maverick.com/blog/austin-free-healthcare-for-the-homeless-art-and-great-music

CHAPTER EIGHT

# Wichita Falls: Aubray, the 'last' drive-through liquor store and the World's Littlest Skyscraper

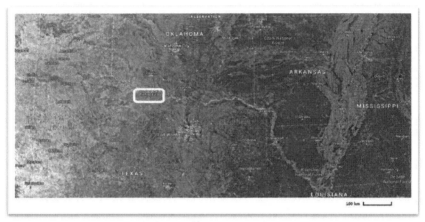

**Wichita Falls (in white oblong)**
*North at top. Imagery ©2017 Landsat/Copernicus, Data SIO, NOAA, U.S. Navy, NGA, GEBCO.*
*Map data ©2017 Google*

I DECIDED that I needed to take a break from the biggest cities while driving, because it takes so long getting in and out of them and it's much easier to get off the Interstate and take a rest stop in more rural areas.

So, I did not even think about going into Dallas.

I had a friend named Aubray, who lived in the small city of Wichita Falls, Texas (not the same as Wichita in Kansas). So, I went to go and catch up with her. I had planned to stay for two nights there.

*Wichita Falls*

*North at top. Imagery ©2017 Google. Map data ©2017 Google*

The last time I'd seen Aubray, she was eating cheap dumplings in a rundown side street restaurant in China. We had got talking and I found her an interesting and inspiring young woman. Aubray was in her twenties and a born-again Christian, very open minded and accepting of people. I loved her interpretation of the Bible, her values and how she treated people. Catching up again in Wichita Falls in late 2016, we discussed the elections and politics in general. She had some friends with her too, and it was interesting to hear what this younger generation thought. They felt that the race relations had got a lot worse recently, and the recession were still affecting a lot of people and towns. Those were some of the reasons why a lot of them were voting Republican this time around. Her friend Kacy told us how she had bought into Obamacare and how the premium cost had increased significantly in the last few years.

Aubray had recently brought a house for quite a reasonable sum of money. She was renovating it and looking at buying something in the inner city as well.

She worked for a company selling organic coffee beans to cafés around Wichita Falls. She would travel over to Oklahoma and sell to stores there too. I hadn't realised how close Wichita Falls was to the border with Oklahoma, it was only about thirty minutes to the border and then another two hours to Oklahoma City.

Aubray, her friend Kacy and another friend named Rachel and I went out to a Mexican restaurant for fajitas. When I ordered, they all laughed because I pronounced it wrong, forgetting the j was an h (more or less)! The meal was amazing. The girls ordered extra jalapeños and chili chocolate.

After that they said they'd take me to one of the last drive-through liquor stores, for the novelty of it I guess. This is a dying institution in view of current social disapproval of drinking and driving, even if in theory you are supposed to wait till you get home. I bought beer, and then we went back to Aubray's house, which she was renovating.

Aubray was an interesting and quirky character. In China, she had told me how she went through a rough patch in her life and that she was going to write a book about it. I thought good on her. She would have a lot of good things to say to people and she is just someone I think everyone likes. Aubray was very open-minded. She told me she didn't care what sexual preferences people had, whether they were gay or straight. She didn't think they should be told they would go to hell for it, and she certainly wasn't going to lecture people on it: no one was perfect so who are we to judge?

Everyone and anyone should be accepted into the church, loved, and not judged. I admired her courage and bravery, which she had oodles of.

The next day, they brought me along with them to see the 'world's littlest skyscraper', more formally the Newby-McMahon Building. The guy who drew the plans did them in inches not feet. He got done for fraud but let off because his investors should have noticed that the plans said inches and not feet before handing over the money. It was a cute little building of red brick and stone built in 1919, and I got a few snaps. We visited a food market in the inner city: they had some brilliant displays. So, I got some photos of those too. Wichita Falls is going through a little bit of a revival at the moment – tourism is taking off.

*Wichita Falls: at the Newby-McMahon Building, the 'littlest skyscraper'*

*Wichita Falls*

*Food markets and shopping cart sculpture*

Wichita Falls only has about 100,000 residents and, yes it does have some nice waterfalls in the Wichita River. Apparently, in the 1800s, the original falls were destroyed by floods, so the city built a new one, which allows the river to flow over steps made on boulders and rock.

We got talking about Obamacare again and it was interesting to hear Aubray's friends' views on Obamacare and how they felt a lot of middle-class Americans were missing out due to the so-called 'subsidy cliff' under which, between 2014 and 2020, the subsidies for insurance fell away once an individual started earning more than about $50,000 a year, quite often in ways that made people worse off for earning more: in some cases a lot worse off, which is why it is called the 'cliff'. A person might jump from paying less than ten per cent of their income to paying more than twenty per cent if their income goes up from $51,000 a year to $52,000 a year currently. I had no idea that this ridiculous element was built into the system: no wonder it had so many critics. Fortunately, the subsidy cliff was abolished by Joe Biden's American Rescue Plan, the third major Covid relief bill to be passed since the outbreak of the pandemic. Though then again, the ARP only abolishes the subsidy cliff for the next two years.

Aubray also told me she has her gun license and carried a gun around with her, because it made her feel safe.

I left after the food market and drove all the way back to Houston. It was quite a nice sunny day. I had hoped to have stopped in Dallas after all, but I failed to take the relevant turnoff due to my non-performing GPS and wasn't too keen on trying any complicated backtracking manoeuvres due to my lack of confidence about driving on the right or as New Zealanders call it, the wrong side of the road. I ended up staying in Woodlands just outside of Houston, pretty much where I had started.

For more, see:

a-maverick.com/blog/wichita-falls-aubray-the-last-drive-through-liquor-store-and-the-worlds-littlest-skyscraper

CHAPTER NINE

# *Way down in New Orleans*

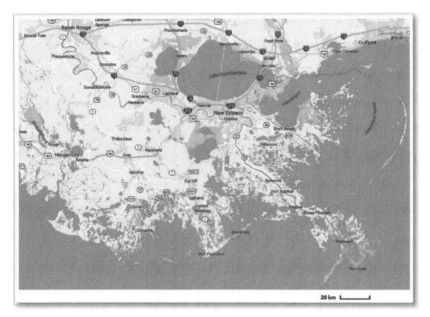

**New Orleans**

*North at top. Map data ©2017 Google, INEGI.*

AFTER Wichita Falls, I was back in Houston and all set to make use of my 45-day Amtrak pass. I had New Orleans in my sights. It was going to be my first experience of a long-distance train ride in the USA, although in truth it was only six hours including the stops along the way.

I liked the train because of all the backyard views you get. I mean, you get to sit back, relax, and watch the scenery pass you by. It is a good opportunity to take photos too. Being on the train really introduced you to America.

I left Houston, Texas with a smile and got on my first train at 12 p.m. I would arrive in New Orleans at six in the evening.

I met a lot of people from New York on that journey. They seemed to love coming on the train rides to the far south, the soulful south. During the ride, I met a group of retirees who were part of a tour group, complete with a tour guide who was escorting them all the way to New Orleans to see the city.

I met a woman who was from the local town of Lafayette, and she said that the recession had really hit that area because the price of oil was so low, and that you could even see in Galveston that they aren't drilling for oil. When the price of oil is low, they just don't bother. It's only when the price is higher, that they do oil exploration.

She told me that in many of the towns in Louisiana people were losing their businesses and the government was doing nothing for them. She said people around the area were not very rich. She indicated to me that people were really struggling. Louisiana depended a lot on oil money.

All I had to do was look out the window and see the derelict housing to know she was right in saying the recession had hit the area hard.

I also met a guy who was a train inspector. He was inspecting the food they were serving on the train that day, which I thought was quite interesting! He told me that several train routes no longer provide cooked food anymore. The food on the train was reasonable: $8 for breakfast and there was a downstairs area with a café section. You could buy peanuts and snack food, salads and pies. And then there was the restaurant. He was looking at the quality of the food and was improving the menu.

*Couple I was talking to over lunch, and woman from Lafayette*

The train went through Lake Charles and passed Lafayette before finally arriving in New Orleans. All along the way we passed rice fields on rice fields, it was amazing. I discovered that crawfish live in the rice fields. Crawfish was the name for freshwater crayfish, smaller than saltwater crayfish or lobsters. We have them in New Zealand, known by the Māori name of kōura, though these are completely different species from the ones in America.

I decided I'd try and find somewhere to buy some and eat it, fresh. The crawfish breed in December in the rice fields and the lady from Lafayette said that the train stopped once because there were flamingos in the rice fields.

As the train pulled into the station, I was really excited. Not that I hadn't enjoyed my train ride – I had – but come on, I was in NEW ORLEANS! This wasn't my first visit to New Orleans. I had been there once before, but that was before Hurricane Katrina, and I hadn't been back since. It had been a long time and I was anxious to see whether the place still had its mojo – a word that came into our language via New Orleans, I believe! I got a bed in a hotel room in the French Quarter. The name of the place that I stayed at was the ISP French Quarter House Hostel, the one and only hostel there too. There was no signage out the front, so it took me a little while to find it.

The hostel was a beautiful two-story villa painted a burnt brown, with a grand staircase to the upper story greeting me in the entrance way. I thought it was quite nice for a hostel. I was going to use Airbnb but the cost of that service in New Orleans was ridiculous, $200 a night!

I got there, sorted myself and my room, and then I hit the town and went to Frenchmen Street and saw some excellent jazz.

I met a couple who were staying in the same hostel, they had both quit their jobs and were going to work in Whistler. He was a great piano player and was playing on one for public use on Frenchmen Street. Only in New Orleans do you have a piano for public use in the street, along with the post boxes and phone booths of a normal city.

*Derelict housing; above-ground graveyard; statue of Italian miracle-worker Padre Pio*

*New Orleans Halloween, bottom photo taken on Frenchmen Street*

The next morning, I did a tour of the city, which also included a look at the devastation still left behind by Hurricane Katrina, which they said was America's most expensive natural catastrophe, the damage in the USA amounting eventually to $125 billion. Over 1,200 people also died in and around New Orleans during Hurricane Katrina, which hit in August 2005. The storm caused damage all the way along the coast from Florida to Texas. There was a huge investigation into the performance of local and federal bodies after the hurricane hit, because of their lack of response, and new books and articles about what some call the 'man-made disaster' and others the 'unnatural disaster' continued to be produced more than a decade later.

The tour guide told us that the houses were being done up and everyone was pretty much sorted. That was not the case. Over ten years afterward, people were still living in condemned houses and still in battles with insurance companies.

More reliably, the guide also informed us that much of New Orleans is below the high tide sea level and there had been a storm surge. The city was between the tidal portion of the Mississippi River and Lake Pontchartrain, protected from both by flood barriers, and the water just went over the top of everything after the flood barriers failed. A later inquiry found that the barriers should have held, but that they were badly designed and built.

An evacuation of the town was supposed to take 36 hours, but you had to have your own transport to leave, and the winds were about 135 miles per hour. Since Hurricane Katrina, the government have said that it is necessary to be about 55 miles outside the city for safe evacuation. People had died because they had fled New Orleans itself but hadn't got far enough away from the low-lying coastal areas that turned into open sea in the storm surge.

The French quarter had come out mostly unscathed, however because it was positioned on the highest point in New Orleans.

One of the saddest things I heard, long-term, was that after Hurricane Katrina 135,000 people left and didn't return.

The tour went around the streets of New Orleans. It showed us the old 'high society' homesteads in the historic Garden District, an area developed in 1832 as a new suburb of wealth. The Garden District has some amazing houses. It is one of the best-preserved areas of colonial mansions in the South.

The old mansions often have high, triple-sash windows that extend from ground level to near the ceiling. It's possible to step in and out through these when they are fully pulled up. People say that triple sash windows were invented to get around a tax on doors, but there's no real evidence for that. It just seems that they were an olden-days equivalent of the modern ranch-slider, often opened right up for ventilation in the muggy climate of New Orleans.

We saw the location of New Orleans' most famous event, the Mardi Gras. This has always been something that interested me, and they had quite a bit of information about that too. During the Mardi Gras, one of the floats is called Muses and they throw away shoes, then you have the Zooloo who throw away coconuts, then the Nikes who do the handbags. So, it is a pretty amazing parade, and I would like to attend it one year!

New Orleans really is a cultural melting pot that exemplifies all things spicy, saucy, vibrant and lively. Everyone seems to be in a permanently good mood, every day is a good one and everyone is in a party mode, in spite of everything. On the tour, they also talked more about the history of New Orleans. The city was named after the Duke of Orléans when it was established by French colonists, at a time when the British had only established themselves, as yet, on the Atlantic coast of North America.

Louisiana became a part of the USA in 1803 by way of the famous Louisiana Purchase, which involved the acquisition of a vast area west of the Mississippi in addition to the present-day State of Louisiana. The whole of that area was named Louisiana at the time, after the French king Louis XIV. It was given that name by a French explorer named

René-Robert Cavelier, Sieur de la Salle, generally known to present-day Americans as de la Salle or La Salle. In fact, this is an error. Sieur de la Salle was an aristocratic title meaning 'master of the hall'. So, renaming Cavelier as La Salle in historical memory is exactly as if some similarly upper-class British explorer, Lord so-and-so, had his title misread as the surname 'Lord'!

Cavelier, or La Salle as he is so erroneously but stubbornly known by the Americans, pops up in the origin stories of many parts of the mid-western USA, from New Orleans all the way up north to Chicago and beyond. In other words, all the parts of the USA that were at one time part of La Salle's historic Louisiana, a territory that extended past Chicago all the way up to modern-day Canada. Whence, all those towns and rivers in that vast region that still have French-sounding names today, names such as Detroit and Des Moines, the Platte River, Bâton Rouge, and so on. They were all named by La Salle or by others who trod in his footsteps.

Many people in New Orleans still speak French. The United States has a French- speaking minority of some one and a half million, with many of them concentrated in and around the modern state of Louisiana. At one time, I had thought that French-speaking populations in North America were confined to Québec, or at any rate to Canada, but this isn't so.

Besides the swinging jazz clubs and music, the sumptuous food and eating places, New Orleans has one of the largest and busiest ports not just in the United States but in the world – something I hadn't learned on my previous trip.

In a stark contrast to the Garden District and French Quarter, there were still a lot of people living in condemned houses in New Orleans. There had been a lot of work done on fixing homes after Hurricane

Katrina, but a lot of people didn't have the money to renovate their homes or have them fixed as they didn't have insurance or were still trying to sort their insurances out and get the companies to pay up. It was a similar situation to one I was already familiar with back home, namely that of Christchurch where, years after the earthquakes of 2010 and 2011, people were still waiting for their insurance companies to pay out. They say it takes a year to get your house rebuilt if it burns down, because of all the paperwork and investigations to make sure you didn't burn it down yourself. And that's just one house. In an urban disaster, it seems that the insurance companies end up being just overwhelmed with arguments over precisely whose fault was that some building did not quite stand up the way that it was supposed to.

So, if the government doesn't step in with some sort of corps of engineers or its equivalent to build a whole lot of new houses straight away, you will still have people living in substandard conditions while arguing the toss with their insurance companies, years later. I wonder whether society was as disorganized in tackling the task of re-housing the masses after World War II as it seems to have been in Christchurch and New Orleans? Or are the ongoing problems of New Orleans and Christchurch just symptoms of present-day free-market economics?

On the evening after the tour, I went to Preservation Hall in Bourbon Street. The audience was a jazz appreciation society, and all these old guys were playing the trombones, the drums and the trumpets. I finally got to try the crawfish and it was outstanding. I did notice a difference in Bourbon Street and Preservation Hall. When I was here earlier, before Katrina, the shops were all mixed and locals used to mingle there, whereas as it now seemed a little overrun with tourists. No doubt that was because so many of the locals had fled, leaving New Orleans to become a sort of museum of its own past, a past which I was fortunate enough to see before Katrina.

*The jester and I; a golden post-box; a stately home in the Garden District*

But this is only relative, not absolute. I found my way to another area that was not as touristy as Bourbon Street, and it was alive with jazz music too, possibly of a more home-made kind. Everyone was playing music in the streets and dancing. I got a photo with someone dressed up as a jester, it was a lot of fun.

I also met this guy who told me he'd been out on a bayou tour earlier that day and the boat was getting a bit close to some of the boat homes of the folk who live deep in the winding estuary inlets (which is what the famous Louisiana word bayou means, from the French), and the people living on the boat fired a few warning shots. That was a bit scary so I decided I would not go on a bayou tour this time. Really though I suppose it's infringing on people's privacy and maybe tour operators should be more respectful, after all it is the bayou-dwellers' home.

*Amtrak 'City of New Orleans' Pin, 2011.*
Wikimedia Commons, Public domain image.

It was Columbus Day that day, too. It was a National Holiday that celebrates the arrival of Christopher Columbus into the Americas in 1492, but it is also celebrated in other countries like Spain and Uruguay.

The second televised debate between Hillary Clinton and Donald Trump occurred on the 9th of October and it was a bit of a shocker. Around this time, everyone watched it and people got put off politics.

No one was impressed, the millennials least of all. I will have a bit more to say about all that a bit later on in the book.

I got myself organised and met some very nice young people at the Hostel in the French Quarter. I relaxed a bit and downloaded the useful Hostel.com app to see how it worked.

Then I got on the City of New Orleans, the train made famous when Arlo Guthrie covered a song about it in 1972, at a quarter to two in the afternoon. At ten o'clock the train rolled on into Memphis, Tennessee, where in the song they change the cars. Memphis was also where this restless rider got off and checked in, at the end of a long day, to a hostel run by a church.

For more, see:

a-maverick.com/blog/way-down-in-new-orleans

CHAPTER TEN

# *Musical Memphis*

I MADE sure I would be off the train for a while in Memphis. It had been an equally long while since I had visited that city. I was eager to see how it had changed as well, and if it had changed as much as New Orleans (hopefully, not). The last time I was there I had done a heap of touristy things, like visit Elvis Presley's grave at Graceland.

On the way, I had passed through Jackson, the capital of the State of Mississippi, and got some photos of it as it went by. Nicknamed 'the city with soul', it was a city I found fascinating even though I was peering at it from a train window.

After that, it was just the train rattling along through green rustic countryside and past small towns and the odd house. Then the city lights of Memphis grew larger on the horizon and the next thing I was rolling into the state of Tennessee at 10 o'clock at night.

I stayed at Pilgrim House Hostel in Memphis, which had no-alcohol policy. That was a relief for me after the hostel I had stayed at in the New Orleans French Quarter. That hostel was crazy and everything and anything happened. Anyway, I found out then that some hostel accommodation apps didn't work, and I was having more success with booking.com and hotels. com on my phone.

Memphis sits on the Mississippi River and has a metro area population of around 1.3 million people. Its most famous citizen, so far, has been Elvis Presley.

In downtown Memphis and New Orleans, their main streets are now used mainly for tourist entertainment. You can't meet the locals in ordinary shops anymore, as you could twenty-odd years ago. Now it's just like one big commercial tourism strip with eateries and nothing else. Queenstown in New Zealand suffers from a similar over-touristification. But if anything, it's more serious in cities famous for their past culture, which gets killed off, whereas Queenstown trades on its scenery.

On the other hand, the renewal and revitalisation of Memphis's inner- city riverfront is amazing, and technology firms have taken root in Memphis as well. There has been a huge uplift since I was there last.

I went to Sun Studios and went on a tour. We were greeted by a bubbly 20-something year old, with bright blonde hair and a wicked smile who was to be our tour guide. She introduced herself as Jayne.

She turned out to be one of the best tour guides I had during the trip, she was just so lively and vibrant and brought the music alive! She was a musician herself and was working on her first album.

It was interesting to compare, say, Johnny Cash as a songwriter, to Elvis who just sang the songs that other people composed. I think there is a definite difference to someone's music when they actually write their own songs. In the studios, they pointed out famous musicians of the past such as Howlin' Wolf! What a name! There was a bit of information about the guy who signed up Elvis, Sam Phillips. He had worked at Sun Studios only for a year before signing up an 18-year-old Elvis Presley who used to sing casually with Jerry Lee Lewis, Johnny Cash, they were all around the same era.

Another place I made it to was called the Stax Museum of American Soul Music. The guide talked about how during the thirties, forties and fifties a lot of African Americans working on the cotton fields moved to Memphis as part of the so-called 'Great Migration' northward, which was triggered by the mechanization of southern farms.

*Sun Records, Memphis*

*The author at Sun Records!*

*Downtown Memphis with urban tramway; paddle steamer*

Memphis at that time was a city with a longstanding musical tradition already, although its early musical traditions had been European. In any case, Memphis stood only just to the north of the Mississippi Delta, a stretch of land between the Mississippi and Yazoo

Rivers in the state of Mississippi where the soil was rich but the people were poor, and still are.

Many ended up in northern cities, but quite a few who were of a musical bent stopped in Memphis.

The Mississippi Delta is where a lot of the really good old-time blues musicians came from ('Delta Blues'). The name is really confusing because the Delta is not the same as the geographical delta of the Mississippi that pokes out into the Gulf of Mexico south of New Orleans.

My hostel was about five kilometres out of downtown Memphis, and I toured the next day with a lot of people. There is a lot of poverty in this area, partly because, in the past, not enough was done to encourage non- agricultural forms of industry in case it attracted workers away from the farms. In fact, industrial development was positively discouraged by local white elites.

One thing that really startled me was a sign I saw along one of the walkways by the river. It was a tribute set out on Thanksgiving to the Native American Tribes who had been wrongfully evicted from the land.

Many of the native tribes who had once lived there were evicted. They called it "The Trail of Tears. The sign was quite a shock to the system, it was heart-breaking.

The native Americans of this area had been known as the Five Civilized Tribes, because they practiced a settled agriculture and lived in towns and villages near the Mississippi and in the American South before the coming of the first Europeans. This way of life has also come to be known as the Mississippian culture. Native Americans of the Mississippian culture had become quite westernised by the 1830s.

Even so, the whites still wanted their land. And so, the settled nations of the Mississippian culture were packed off to modern-day Oklahoma to live among buffalo-hunting tribes, who in their turn were starved out when the whites started shooting all their buffalo from trains for what was misnamed as sport – but that's another railway story.

To round off the story of my second visit to Memphis, there were also tours you could do on the river. But I had done that before, and I decided to head on up to Chicago.

For more, see:

a-maverick.com/blog/musical-memphis

CHAPTER ELEVEN

# *Chicago: Violence and architecture*

**Chicago Regional Context, including Milwaukee and Minneapolis**
North at top. ap data ©2017 Google

I DO like Chicago, the lakeside city in the state of Illinois. The vibe, the musicals, the hustle and bustle of almost ten million people and then the glimmering city lights on Lake Michigan. Everything about it is completely wondrous: it's no wonder Chicago is a star attraction on the list of US cities for tourists.

Chicago rose to prominence as a processing centre for livestock in the original cowboy era, the generation or so after the American Civil War. Cattle were driven (and later, sent by rail) from pastures in places such as Texas, Oklahoma and Kansas to be butchered on an industrial scale in Chicago, and the meat then sent out to all the cities of the populous eastern states in insulated railway cars which were packed with ice.

Along with the fact that Chicago was located halfway between the Wild West cattle-herders and their eastern markets, an abundance of water, and cold local winters that made it possible to harvest huge amounts of ice, were the other reasons why Chicago was a good place for the meat-packing trade to flourish in the days before mechanical refrigeration had been perfected.

The city was rebuilt after a notorious 1873 fire. Twenty years after the fire, a World's Fair was attended by 23 million people. The Chicago World's Fair of 1893 showcased the massed use of electric lights for the first time in a great display of illumination that came to be called the 'White City'. A visionary 1909 plan by Daniel Burnham and Edward H. Bennett gave further shape to Chicago. And the city had more than its share of heroic public works as well.

For instance, in 1900, the flow of the Chicago River was reversed down a newly created ship canal in order to keep Lake Michigan and the city environs pure. Only a low ridge, less than five metres high, stood between the watershed of Lake Michigan and the watershed of the Mississippi River. The increasingly polluted Chicago River flowed sluggishly through almost flat terrain into the lake, with pollution observably making it as far as Chicago's drinking water inlet, located two miles out in the lake at the time, in 1885.

The reversal of the river toward the Mississippi flushed the city's wastes, including the effluvium of its many slaughterhouses and stockyards, into what is still called the Chicago Sanitary and Ship Canal. The canal made it possible to link the Great Lakes to the Gulf of Mexico via the Mississippi, which is dredged to a depth of at least 9 feet (2.7 metres) all the way up to St Paul, Minnesota, for barge navigation. At the same time, a tremendous and unceasing flow of water out of Lake Michigan via the canal, and its length (28 miles or 45 kilometres), diluted the sewage and slaughterhouse waste to a degree considered acceptable by the standards of the time.

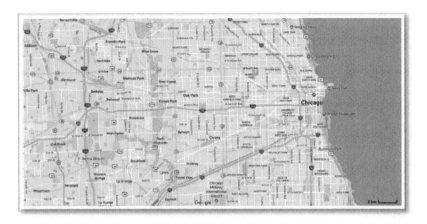

*Chicago city area*

North at top. Map data ©2017 Google

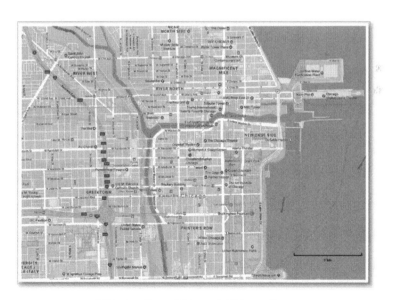

*Chicago Central City with Chicago River*

North at top. Map data ©2017 Google

*Replica of the 1893 Statue of the Republic, Jackson Park, Chicago*

From Adrian Gamble, 'The World of Tomorrow . . . Today: Revisiting 3 World Fair and Expo Sites', 10 May 2016, on skyrisecities.com: 'image by Flickr user Christa Lohman via Creative Commons'

It thus became possible to tow barges from the Great Lakes all the way down to Galveston via Chicago, increasing Chicago's importance even further.

When I was there, Chicago was a 'sanctuary city', meaning that its officials turned a blind eye to illegal immigrants. Sanctuary cities justified this policy on the grounds that illegal immigrants from countries such as Mexico (thought to number about eleven million across the USA) would be more likely to lead law-abiding lives and enrol their children properly in school, vaccinate their children, and so on, if they did not in fact fear deportation as a consequence of coming into contact with local officials. In effect, sanctuary cities took the view that federal immigration laws were as unworkable and socially harmful as Prohibition: a policy that led to the level of gangsterism with which the Chicago of the 1920s and 1930s was so notoriously associated.

The name Chicago is thought to refer to an abundance of wild garlic, known in current native American spelling from this region as shikaakwa. The explorer René-Robert Cavelier, Sieur de La Salle, was the first European known to have recorded Chicago as a placename, spelt Chécagou, in 1679.

Soldiers, trappers and farmers followed, and in 1830 a pioneering town was founded; a town that officially became a city on 4 March 1837. Chicago boomed into the third most populous metropolitan area in the USA after greater Los Angeles and greater New York. The population of greater Chicago today is almost ten million people.

I feel privileged to have visited Chicago. But, while I love the city I don't look at things through rose-tinted glasses either. Everything has its negatives and downsides too.

I was staying at the Freehand hostel in the inner city for about 80 dollars a night. Freehand had a great range of facilities and was quite upmarket for that price.

I walked around the popular hub at Navy Pier and got some good snaps of the skyline at sunset – gorgeous! The streets are clean, and the city has a well-thought-out skyline where buildings cannot block other people's views.

Youth under eighteen need adult company around the city and by the river after certain times at night! I liked this idea – it makes sense! I like that you have to be twenty-one years of age to purchase alcohol in the USA, not eighteen years of age like at home in New Zealand. Signs also prohibit cyclists from riding in pedestrian areas.

Regrettably, some of the public order issues in Chicago are more serious than that. Chicago has a history of violence, including murderous 'race riots' in 1919, which were really a pogrom against the city's African Americans and something that happened in a lot of other cities in the USA at around that time.

And the Chicago-gangster era of the 1920s and 1930s, fuelled by the profits of illicit booze-brewing and smuggling from Canada in the Prohibition era. As with the city's legitimate industries, the fact that Chicago is a national transportation hub also made it the northern hub of the illicit booze trade.

In recent years, the city also gained the nickname of 'Chiraq' for its very high rate of gun violence, an echo of the 1930s organised-crime gangster era, except that now they are called 'gangstas', and aren't so organised.

Often there are several shootings a day, dozens over a weekend. Over the July 4th weekend in 2017, more than a hundred people were shot in Chicago. There were 762 killings in 2016 in Chicago, a nearly

60% rise on 2015, and it is estimated that gunshot wounds in the city cost $2.5 billion a year to treat.

Part of the problem is that while Chicago, like Los Angeles and New York, has strict gun-control laws, the city is surrounded by other states and even parts of Illinois that have lax gun-control laws. The city of Gary, Indiana, where gun ownership is much more loosely regulated, almost abuts Chicago, and gang members have no trouble obtaining guns there and smuggling them into Chicago. Still, it is obviously a syndrome with many causes. Tightening up the gun laws in Gary would surely be only the first step toward getting Chicago's culture of violence under control.

On a brighter note, the latest buildings include environmentally sustainable air conditioning through a chilled water system operated by a firm called Enwave Chicago. A company produces chilled water at five strategically located downtown Chicago plants, where they pump chilled water through a trench for miles underground. The chilled water is generated using environmentally sustainable techniques, which in Chicago mostly consist of the slow melting of ice frozen in winter and stored in giant blocks for summer.

*Chicago Skyline*

*The Chicago River and the local Trump Tower*

The river has lots of bridges over it, each a short distance apart

In Toronto, Enwave employs the even more interesting method of drawing near-freezing water from the deep bottom of Lake Ontario for the city's water supply and using the coldness of this deep water to cool the CBD on the way to the water treatment plant. Unfortunately, Lake Michigan is too shallow at the south end near Chicago, the headwater end of the lake that has normally drained north, for that to work.

For more, see:

a-maverick.com/blog/chicago-violence-and-architecture

## CHAPTER TWELVE

# *Milwaukee to Montana: 28 hours on a train*

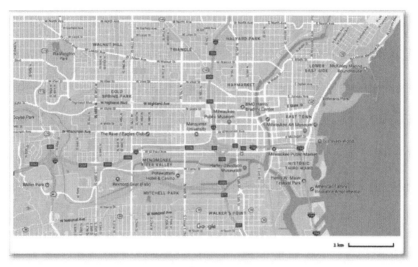

*Milwaukee*

North at top. Map data ©2017 Google

AFTER the great city of Chicago, I was headed on a short stretch of railway line to Milwaukee. It was only two hours, and the train was pretty busy!

Milwaukee is in the state of Wisconsin, somewhat further north on Lake Michigan.

I stayed outside of the main city in a place called the Crowne Plaza. I visited the Milwaukee Art Museum and saw an amazing display of American photographic art from the 1960s: a new era really. They had also encapsulated the modern art from around the world based on the theme of Pablo Picasso, which was unique.

*Milwaukee, 3D aerial from lakeshore, showing street grid and avenues*
Imagery ©2017 Google, TerraMetrics. Map data ©2017 Google

I got a taxi back to my accommodation and had a good conversation with the driver. She was quite happy to talk to me about her life, she was a single mother of two children who only earned $500 a week. That may sound fine to some but let's put it into perspective, on average an apartment in Milwaukee costs $1225 a month.

Milwaukee was an interesting town, but it was time to gear up and get ready for a whopping 28 hours on the train, the Empire Builder. The Empire Builder is a passenger train run from Chicago towards the Pacific coast as part of the Great Northern Railway circuit.

On the ride from Milwaukee to West Glacier in Montana, where I planned to get off, I met this professional guy who lived in Milwaukee. We discussed homelessness there and he told me every day he was confronted by homeless people, and he couldn't afford to give money all the time. So, what he and his friends did was they got together and started giving them food, and he always gave them a bottle of water and a granola bar.

*Milwaukee Art Museum*

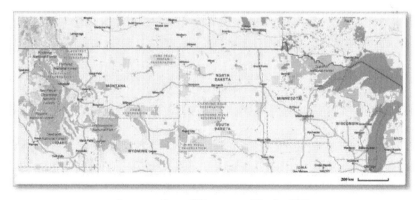

*Journey from Chicago to Glacier NP*

*North at top. Map data ©2017 Google*

*Boarding the Empire Builder Train, Chicago to Seattle (or Portland); Lake Michigan from the Train*

I mentioned to him that I had noticed some racial tensions and he agreed saying that he thought, "Milwaukee was a very segregated town." I've heard that a few times from the locals I spoke to, as well.

In fact, Milwaukee has the odd distinction of being the most segregated big city in the USA even though it is almost as far north as

Canada and located in the historically progressive state of Wisconsin, known a hundred years ago as the leading 'social laboratory' of the United States.

Rolling on through Minnesota and the Dakotas on the way to Montana was interesting, with some very stunning scenery. One thing that hit me as we travelled through all these towns was the emptiness of some areas, particularly outside of Milwaukee. Complete towns that just looked uninhabited.

There were trains with 300 carriages picking up grain from farms with silos. It was amazing to see. I was also amazed at all the oil being extracted and transported by train. This is obviously why there is the pressure to build the controversial Dakota Access Pipeline (DAPL). People fear the DAPL will leak and pollute groundwater and have been protesting against it on those grounds; but on the other hand, when the oil is being transported by railway cars, which derail from time to time, there is always the chance of a fiery and fatal inferno of the kind that happened in Lac Mégantic in Québec in 2014. Rail is an inferior method of transportation in every way for a dangerous liquid that is going to be consumed in huge quantities every day. I guess the real issue in the whole DAPL dispute, which I'll be getting to shortly, is whether America should be trying to expand oil production in the first place in view of climate change.

The twin cities of Minneapolis-Saint Paul straddled two states. A same- sex couple I met on the train told me that the twin cities were the coldest in the United States! They were also among the most gay-friendly. I wanted to visit them, but I wasn't going to have time since the national parks out west were about to reduce their hours and services for winter. I wanted to get the western parks before that happened. So, I went straight through.

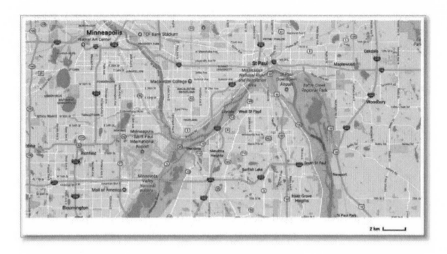

*Minneapolis—St Paul*
North at top. Map data ©2017 Google

It was interesting to be a passive viewer through my window, watching towns slide by. Some thriving, and others not so much. I stared out the window for most of the morning.

That train ride through the Dakotas was fascinating, as you could see all the drilling rigs puncturing the landscape. Surrounding them in blank vast countryside there were buildings and rough makeshift camps for the workers. A woman told me her son had told her not to get off anywhere near Willeston in South Dakota. The roughnecks there were extra-rough, apparently.

I met a guy on his way to Portland, Oregon. He told me that in the old days the government had offered free land to anyone prepared to plant trees because there hadn't been any trees when the first settlers arrived, just windswept lonesome prairie. The first settlers were called sodbusters, because they built their houses out of blocks of dirt, and there hadn't been much to burn to keep warm in the thirty-below winters either.

I also met a couple who had retired from Michigan. She was a teacher, who said that teachers had great retirement plans. There was a group of thirty ex-teachers who were being led by a tour guide on the train. They were going to Seattle as part of a tour all over the US, which was pretty amazing. They were in Sleeper Class. She said that her husband suffered from diabetes and so that made it hard for them to travel to other countries.

It really is amazing who you do meet on the train, I mean in the course of 28 hours sitting on one you do strike up some interesting conversations. I met a guy from Seattle whose parents had moved to Dakota, who said there were no employment opportunities. He said there were only two seasons, winter and summer, and nothing in between. He said his daughter liked the four seasons of more regular parts and wouldn't want to live there.

*The author asleep on the train, North Dakota (or thereabouts)*

As in most other parts of the USA, Amtrak did not own the train tracks in this region. It was not unusual for the Empire Builder to be around ten hours late because some freight train or oil train had been given priority.

I wasn't really impressed with all the oil drilling, now that climate change is for real. There were a few people talking about the protests against the DAPL at Standing Rock Reservation, which caught my attention.

The guy from Seattle told me that Montana would have an interesting election outcome – that they tended to vote one way for the Senate and another way for the House of Representatives, and that they always put a dollar each way.

The scenery was stunning, I mean it almost felt unreal, looking at it all slide by like a diorama behind a glass panel. It was quite a harsh and dry looking landscape, but I loved it.

I got a bit tired of being on the train and was itching to get off and go wandering through the natural beauty of Montana. People talked about the danger of bears and the like, but I had already thought that I would go trekking in Montana, no matter what.

I got off at the Whitefish Amtrak Station, near Glacier National Park. I didn't want to stay in camping accommodation, which is why I got off at Whitefish, the largest and most organized town in those parts.

When I arrived, there were people waiting at the stations to catch trains that were up to 20 hours late! This was all due to slips, freight trains and not having the right of way. We had had to wait for freight trains as well, but fortunately it had never taken that long.

For more, see:

a-maverick.com/blog/milwaukee-to-montana-28-hours-on-a-train

CHAPTER THIRTEEN

# Glacier National Park: Grizzly bears and being growled at, in one of the last wild places

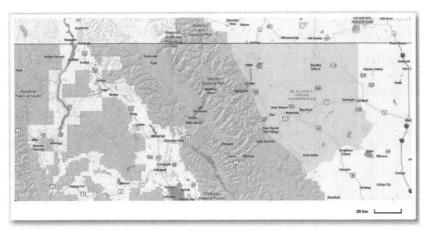

**Glacier National Park and Blackfeet Reservation**
*North at top. Map data ©2017 Google*

WHITEFISH is one of those places where snow-capped mountains dominate the horizon. It was refreshing to be somewhere free of tall buildings, concrete and noise.

Whitefish is also home base for the Glacier National Park, Flathead National Forest, and Big Mountain. The area boosts a popular ski resort and ski-field. It is also home to bears. Lots of bears.

I found Whitefish very similar to my second hometown of Queenstown in New Zealand. I found a hostel in Whitefish and booked myself into a shared room. That's where I met a guy called Gabriel, a salsa dancer. When he found out I was going to Cuba next,

115

he wanted to meet me there. I laughed at his forthcomingness and simply said, "We will see". I don't tend to plan too much when I travel – I mean, I just see where my feet will take me.

I told him about Queenstown, and he said he had long wanted to get there at some stage. For work and travel. He had worked as a chef and travelled all around the world.

The hostel I stayed in was great, so much nicer than the Airbnb places I had had to put up with. The hostel's owners were nice people, a couple of sisters. They said that they had noticed the downturn in the oil industries too.

There were a few other people I met staying in the hostel and around town. Many of them had finished up work in Alaska and had come to Whitefish for work there, or over in the Glacier National Park.

*Dancing Bears Inn, East Glacier Park*

Talking to them made me really want to go to Alaska, no question about it. I have been talked into visiting a place called Juneau. I'll get there in the near future, I hope.

You can do bear camp expeditions, where they take you out into the wild and you go looking for bears. The other, somewhat safer option is to get a helicopter or plane ride over the area to see them—which I think would be incredible.

I was going to head to Glacier National Park next, only an hour and a half away from Whitefish. I went to the local grocery store and stocked up on food and bought cooking utensils and walking sticks as well. I had to stop eating out because everything was a bit expensive here. So anyway, I decided to buy a whole lot of stuff. I planned to have just one meal a day out and then make my own breakfast and lunch.

I visited the Blackfoot reservation, where I was surprised to find a casino. But I shouldn't have been, because that is how a lot of reservations make extra income in actual fact. Under the old Indian Treaties, many of the laws that were applied to other Americans didn't apply on reservations. Somebody figured out that this included laws against casinos as well: at one time banned nearly everywhere in the USA except Nevada. And that's how the whole reservation-casino thing got started as well.

I was really excited about getting to the Glacier National Park: it was something straight out of *National Geographic*. Sheer beauty.

I hired a rental car and had to double check my travel insurances. Luckily, I didn't have to pay extra because I was insured for damaging a car and car accidents, so that was good news.

I find it better to do online searches, but the funny thing about my rental car was that it didn't have GPS which was crazy. You most definitely need one out here. So, I ended up using different SIMs for GPS.

My NZ SIM only got 300 MB and my US one had 2 GB, but I think it had already run out.

I was told to get an annual pass for entering the parks for about $80, which is more than reasonable. Someone else could use it after me, I thought.

From Whitefish, I went to the township of West Glacier inside the park. At this time of year, the bears are getting ready for hibernation and eating a lot, so you have to be very, very careful. You can get bear spray which apparently keeps them away. I didn't know any of this, but there were a lot of people on the trails that I did, so I felt safe in the belief that the bears would stay away. There were also mountain lions, but I didn't know a lot about them.

As I would later find out, mountain lions are perhaps even more dangerous than bears overall, because they have the ability to stalk lone hikers in perfect silence, biding their time till the hiker is on a particularly lonesome section of the trail and then pouncing.

A boy I spoke to later told me that he had heard of a mountain biker who was attacked by a mountain lion, and that it was having a real go at him, and he managed to get back on his bike and took off and the mountain lion chased him like a creature out of a nightmare till he came across two women. The women threw rocks at the lion till it left all three of them alone.

You'd relive that in your dreams for a while, I am sure; pedaling till the sheets are all over the place!

I also found out, later on, that mountain lions are not closely related to lions. Even though they are called lions, they are really more like a giant version of the domestic cat. Like the domestic cat they are very loose- limbed and agile, and amazingly good at jumping. But loose joints mean that housecats and mountain lions find running to be very exhausting, like running through sand, even though they can go fast for a short time. This makes house cats and mountain lions 'lazy'. They would rather hunt by slow stalking and an eventual pounce than by giving serious chase like a true lion, let alone a cheetah, or a wolf. The mountain lion that chased the mountain biker was probably more out of breath than he was by the time the women started throwing rocks at it.

Many pet dogs disappear thanks to mountain lions, which sometimes venture into suburban areas. Mountain lions also used to be killed by farmers in great numbers, because, of course, no farmer's sheep was safe from their depredations.

People told me that of all the common animals, only domestic cats were too intelligent to be taken by mountain lions. I don't know that cats are smarter than dogs in general; but they probably are wiser to the mountain lion's sneaky habits, in this instance, than dogs would be. Perhaps the mountain lion also recognizes a kindred spirit, as well.

I think that's one thing about living in New Zealand: we are liable a little naïve about the outdoors in other countries. The most dangerous native animal we have is a venomous spider that no one I know has ever seen in the wild! This is the Katipo, a relative of Australia's Redback. Hardly anyone has ever been bitten by a Katipo and I don't think anyone has ever actually died from the effects, or at least, been proven to have done so.

So, I set off without too much concern on the Trail of the Sealers and on a nature walk within the West Glacier section, reading all the signs saying 'Watch out for Bears', what to do if you encounter one and where to store your food. They had lots of bear-proof containers around the park where you can put your food. But it all seemed manageable to me.

I was told to sing loudly to keep the bears and mountain lions away, so I did, in between laughing at the incongruity of it.

*Glacier National Park*

*The place where I went walking*

*East Glacier Park sign*

*East Glacier Park: Blackfeet Statue and Native American-themed road underpass (in background)*

For more, see:

a-maverick.com/blog/glacier-national-park-grizzly-bears-and-being-growled-at-in-one-of-the-last-wild-places

CHAPTER FOURTEEN

# *The amazing wildlife of Yellowstone and its comeback*

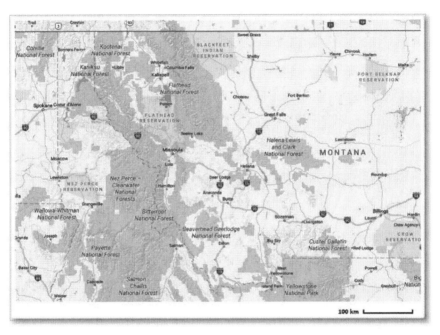

*Glacier National Park and part of Yellowstone National Park*
*North at top. Map data ©2017 Google*

YELLOWSTONE National Park is almost nine thousand square kilometres in area. It straddles the three states of Montana, Wyoming and Idaho.

I was in West Yellowstone, in the state of Montana just west of the national park. I wanted to visit the Grizzly and Wolf Discovery Center, a not- for-profit wildlife education centre.

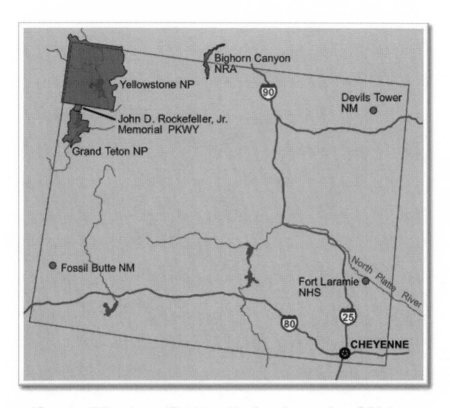

*The state of Wyoming, outlined in red in the colour version of this image, with the Yellowstone and Grand Teton national parks toward the top left.*

Wikimedia Commons, NPS public domain. North rotated slightly clockwise from top.

*Deer and Bison*

*A Mountain River*

*Mammoth Hot Springs*

Yellowstone is famous for its rugged natural beauty, cascading waterfalls, sky-high mountains and rocky cliff faces. It's also home to many animals and birds, including wolves, bison, and of course, grizzly bears.

Native American people have lived in the Yellowstone National Park for over 11,000 years, so there are plenty of historical sites there as well.

High up in the mountain areas grow the whitebark pine trees, an iconic symbol of Yellowstone. I had heard that they were dying off in mass amounts. I thought the Discovery Center would help shed some light on this for me.

The Discovery Center was a great experience, and an awesome way for me to see the wolves and grizzly bears up close – but safely. I admired the commitment the staff had to conservation: they were working on lots of programs.

And so, I continued on to the Lamar Valley and its wildlife. Hopefully, I thought, I will see some of the animals and get some good photos! And I did! But fortunately, before I left through the North Entrance and its historic Roosevelt Arch (named after Theodore Roosevelt, not the other one), I came across the Mammoth Hot Springs, where silica terraces reminded me of the fabled Pink and White Terraces of New Zealand's Rotorua Region.

The latter were briefly a Yellowstone-like tourist attraction until a huge volcanic eruption buried them in 1886. The risk of volcanic eruptions is something that goes with this sort of geothermal territory in New Zealand and America alike. I should add, by the way, that the Mammoth Hot Springs were only a part of Yellowstone's geothermal wonderland, other parts of which, as with Rotorua, are more colourful: painted rainbow colours by red and green algae, yellow sulfur, and clear blue water.

So, get in and see those sights while they are there, they might not be there next year!

For more, see:

a-maverick.com/blog/the-amazing-wildlife-of-yellowstone-
and-its-comeback

## CHAPTER FIFTEEN

# *Grand Tetons: The Ho-Hum Motel and the crazy cat lady*

WITH travelling you always get the good and the bad, I mean obviously from my experiences with Airbnb they can be a little all over the show. You never know what you might get. Then there are the funny stories, the ones you can laugh about for many months and years to come.

I don't know whether it was the name of the Ho-Hum Motel in West Yellowstone that caught my attention and sparked my curiosity, or the sign that claimed, "your next stop for comfort". So, I went into make a booking and was immediately hit with the smell of cat pee. It stunk really bad. And then this older lady appeared behind the counter. I bit my lip not to laugh, and let her take my booking for a room.

This was some years ago, of course: it might be quite different now! Anyhow, she was an interesting person; it turned out she was the mother of the town's mayor. And didn't care too much what people thought of her cats.

It was only $50 a night and quite clean. The crazy cat lady's cats hadn't left their mark beyond reception, so that was all good. It was cheap, which was great: my other option would have been a tent and that would have been far too cold.

My next stop on the list was the Grand Teton National Park, in Wyoming.

This was the opportunity of a lifetime: I had always wanted to go there.

*Grand Teton range information board, and the range itself*

Grand Teton National Park is amazing. I mean really amazing: jaw-dropping spectacular scenery. Its focal point is the oddly shaped peak called Grand Teton, said to have been named after the French word for teat or nipple, which reaches an altitude of 13,775 feet (4,199 metres). This national park has beautiful crystal-clear lakes, framed by rugged triangular snow-covered peaks, and I fell in love with it immediately.

I did a three-hour walk and got some photos of the Native Americans who lived in the area. I didn't spend a lot of time there unfortunately: definitely not as much as I would have liked to. So, I spent the night in the Ho-Hum Motel and then spent the next day driving the eight hours back down to Whitefish to catch the Seattle train at 10 p.m. that night.

I was off on a twelve-hour train ride, through some of the most beautiful countryside I had yet seen once the sun came up. It was thoroughly enjoyable, even if it was a fair chunk of time to spend getting to Seattle, only to spend about 36 hours there before moving on to the next port of call.

For more, see:

a-maverick.com/blog/grand-tetons-the-ho-hum-motel-and-the-crazy-cat-lady

## CHAPTER SIXTEEN

# The Clean Skies of Seattle

I WAS only going to be in Seattle for 36 hours. I found a place in 2nd Street in the City Hostel in Seattle. Seattle is a sprawling metropolis and the largest city in the state of Washington. It was founded in 1852.

When I arrived, it was raining torrentially. This is apparently quite normal. But the city is also famous for the clear blue skies that come after, with no dust or haze.

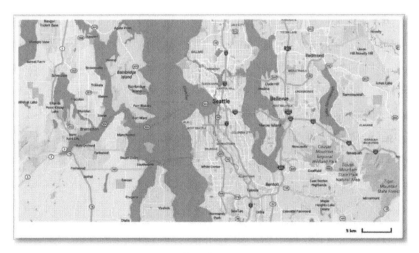

**Seattle area**
North at top. Map data ©2017 Google

Thankfully, the weather settled down enough for me to do a walking tour of the city. This was an organized tour, after which you gave a donation at the end of what you thought it was worth. A typically eccentric, US West Coast way of doing things!

We went around for two hours, and I was told all about the history of the city. Seattle was named after the local Native American Chief of the Duwamish tribe, whose name is spelt Si'ahl in modern Duwamish spelling. Other variants of his name that survive in local placenames include Sealth, as in Camp Sealth

Chief Seattle, or Si'ahl, was born around 1786 and lived until 1866. He got along well with the early American settlers, which is why they named the city after him. Seattle was originally a logging town, and the settlers chopped down hundreds of one- and two-thousand-year-old trees on the site of the modern city. It's not clear what Chief Seattle thought about that. The well-known environmental sermon supposedly given by Chief Seattle in 1854 called 'This Earth is Precious', which ends in the words "the end of living and the beginning of survival," and which appears in whole or in part on many a hippie-type poster, actually comes from the script of a historical drama penned by the Hollywood screenwriter Ted Perry; a soliloquy that Perry himself later came to regard as corny and patronising.

The food was amazing in Seattle; I could get a decent seafood meal for about $10. One I vividly remember was wild salmon chowder with prawns. It was delicious! There has been a huge boost in the number of restaurants over the last few years, and they are encouraging people to eat there with happy hours and things, like that so it's a great environment. It's good for the economy because there is a lot of competition. It's all really good.

*Monument to Chief Si'ahl; Seattle Art Museum; drain cover with map of down-town cast into it; woman from Germany on Seattle walking tour.*

Seattle has an incredible music industry. The city has been the stepping-stone for many famous rock bands including Nirvana, Pearl Jam and Alice in Chains. There is a lot of theatre and live music all around the inner city which makes it a great place for a night out.

The waterfront of Seattle is amazing. There is huge change going on there and an eco-park being built. They are removing the Alaskan Way freeway and putting it underground, which makes it more pedestrian friendly.

There was a huge fire in 1889 which destroyed the whole central district. A lot of the inner city still consists of the brick buildings that replaced the wooden buildings immediately after the fire. These had a style similar to what I had seen in Vancouver.

I went to Pike Place Market, where the very first ever Starbucks café was opened in 1971. This old and famous market was renovated in the same decade by the local architect and heritage conservationist Victor Steinbrueck, who also designed the city's famous Space Needle.

On the western outskirts of the city there are the amazing Olympic Mountains, where they have a lot of skiing and snowboarding events.

To the southeast is the highest and most famous mountain in Washington State, Mount Rainier, a huge volcano which has a reputation as one of the most potentially dangerous volcanoes in the world in terms of its size, likelihood of eruption and mudflows, and proximity to a big city. In the meantime, it is a hive of outdoor activities and winter sports as well.

I managed to catch a ferry out to Bainbridge Island, which was full of trees turning the rich hues of autumn. There was this friendly girl from Germany who was in a wheelchair and travelled around the world on her own. She was so inspiring!

I did see some indigenous art works in the museums which was great too. One thing I wonder about is why so many place names in North America seem to be English-language ones which are often banal and endlessly recycled, while the indigenous ones have vanished from the landscape. This is true even in the Pacific Northwest, which is otherwise proud of its indigenous heritage. Just about all the placenames in Seattle are English-sounding.

A little further south, Portland, Oregon, is named after Portland, Maine, which is in turn named after Portland, in England. And then there are all the Sunnyvales and Fruitvales, in Auckland and northern California alike. Explorers with a naval background like Captains Cook and, for that matter, Vancouver, were like John Milton by comparison: fond of names like Disappointment, Deception, Obstruction, Foulwind and Flattery. Even so, the indigenous names are still lost in such cases.

Indigenous place names are better preserved, in the original language, in New Zealand than in many parts of North America. This is perhaps because of the somewhat better shape in which Māori indigenous culture survived, as well as the early formalization of Māori as a written language. When the main body of colonists arrived New Zealand already had Māori place-names which were written down on maps and in deeds. New Zealand is like Hawai'i in that respect.

Marijuana is decriminalised in Seattle: you can buy it but you can't smoke it in public.

Seattle introduced a minimum wage of $15 about three years ago, to be phased in progressively, which I thought was interesting. Certainly, the economists think so and its effects are being closely studied.

I was busy organising my trip to Yosemite National Park, so I was a bit preoccupied with that, I think I saw most of the things I needed to in Seattle. So that was all fine, and it was time I got on my way again.

I could have caught the train all the way to Merced, the gateway to Yosemite. But with all the stops and changing trains, that would have taken 24 hours: far too long! And so, it made sense to take a break part-way in San Francisco, where they say the future happens first.

For more, see:

a-maverick.com/blog/the-clean-skies-of-seattle

**Note:** In 1993, Nancy Zussy, at that time the State Librarian of Washington State, wrote a letter describing the evolution of successively more apocryphal versions of Chief Seattle's January 1854 speech, which first appeared in a newspaper in quite a different form to the Perry version in 1887, its publication delayed for some reason by more than thirty years. As of the time of writing, you can access Ms Zussy's essay on:

synaptic.bc.ca/ejournal/wslibrry.htm#.WYU404SGOM9

CHAPTER SEVENTEEN

# *San Francisco: Utopia, Limited*

*San Francisco and its approaches, north at top above, and as seen from the air and from the west below*

*Imagery ©2017 Data SIO, NOAA, U.S. Navy, NGA, GEBCO, Landsat/Copernicus, Data CSUMB SFML, CA OPC, Google. Map data x©2017 Google.*

AND so, I caught the plane down to San Francisco, the progressive city in northern California where it is sometimes said that the future happens first.

Greater San Francisco is home to the excellent Bay Area Rapid Transit or BART system, one of the few brand-new public transport systems built in mid-twentieth-century America. BART was the product of a temporarily utopian vision of what the future city would be like.

Computer-controlled, running on mostly overhead tracks, BART began service in 1972. The early BART A-series trains from the late 1960s are streamlined and painted white and still look futuristic today, in the way that a Stanley Kubrick movie from that era does. There is also a separate metro system within the downtown and inner-suburbs part of San Francisco, called 'Muni'.

It's always great to be back in San Fran. Even so, I was feeling really tired, and I was only spending one night there before heading on to Yosemite National Park.

I ended up in the International Hostel in San Francisco, which was very clean and had plenty of lounges and seating everywhere. That was great. But it also had a bit of a congregation of people, locals I think, who had no money.

Large numbers of poor and homeless people have converged on California, apparently because it isn't so cold in winter as the northern states, nor as punitive as the Old South.

Anyway, I couldn't get to sleep for ages because my roommate kept talking to me. I got up early in the morning and I ran into a guy who told me he was a drug dealer and had got caught up in some bad things.

The city definitely had its seedy side. At the same time housing costs were the highest in the USA, higher even in Auckland, which was saying something.

San Francisco: BART A-car at the Oakland Coliseum Stadium, 22 August 2013, public domain image by Maurits90, driver dodged for this book to render more conspicuous; photos of San Francisco Arts Commission posters; the Golden Gate Bridge.

Workers in the high-tech industries can't afford to live there and want housing to be provided socially. So much for the West Coast Utopia, which needs to have its social arrangements brought into line with its technological promise.

People thought I was homeless myself because I had a backpack. So, after a while I caught a bus to Emeryville on the Oakland side of the Bay, and from there I got the San Joaquins train to Merced, which is just outside of Yosemite National Park.

I could have got a bus all the way to Yosemite National Park, but then I wouldn't have had as much freedom to get around. I decided to hire a car there for $34 a day so I could go where I wanted and when.

For more, see:

**a-maverick.com/blog/san-francisco-utopia-limited**

CHAPTER EIGHTEEN

# *Yosemite: The park that has trouble with names*

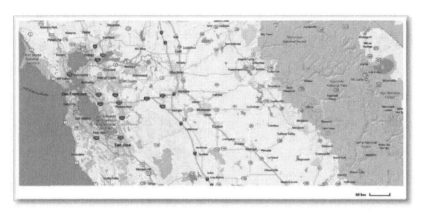

*San Francisco and the Yosemite area. Yosemite National Park is part of the area of contiguous parklands shown as a broad green belt in the map above (north at top). Map data ©2017 Google.*

I PICKED up my rental car in Merced and drove through the rain to Yosemite National Park: a three-hour trip in view of the winter weather.

Yosemite National Park goes back more than 100 years as a park and has a much longer geographical and cultural history. The first people to reside in the area were there over 6,000 years ago. In the nineteenth century, the inhabitants were called the Ahwahnechee, which translates in English to the people of Ahwahnee, meaning a valley that resembles a gaping mouth. This is a reference to the spectacular entrance to what we now call the Yosemite Valley. It comes from the language of the Miwok people, of whom the Ahwanechee were a sub-group.

*Above: Albert Bierstadt (1865),* Looking Down Yosemite Valley, California: *in the Birmingham Museum of Art, Birmingham, Alabama. Public Domain image from Wikimedia Commons.*

*Below: Photo take by myself looking up the valley.*

Yosemite is not the most ideal name for the locality. It comes from a word meaning a band of killers or renegades, an unflattering term for the Ahwahnechee that circulated among their tribal enemies in the 1840s.

The Ahwahnechee had been scattered to the four winds and absorbed by other Miwok clans because of the outbreak of a mysterious plague in the valley sometime around 1800: probably a European disease to which the Ahwahnechee would have had no immunity.

By the time of the California gold rush in 1849, the tribe had re-formed and reoccupied the valley. However, their tribal enemies claimed that the refounded Ahwahnechee weren't the real thing anymore but just a sort of gang, a motley bunch of outcasts from the various other Miwok clans which had appropriated the name of the old and honourable Ahwahnechee tribe. White settlers in the gold rush era, the 'forty-niners', appropriated the term Yosemite, as they spelt it, in the mistaken beliefs that it (a) meant tribe of the grizzly bear rather than band of killers, and (b) was the true name of the Ahwahnechee, with whom the gold-seekers had come into conflict themselves. This conflict didn't last very long. But nobody bothered to change the name to anything more PC before Yosemite became too well known to change.

And so, we're stuck with a name that might be a gross calumny against an unfortunate group of plague survivors. Whatever we call the place, Yosemite is designated a World Heritage Site and sees millions of tourists a year. The very first tourist group arrived in 1865, and since then its natural landscape and stunning scenery have captivated people from all corners of the globe. I was going to become one of them.

*Trail signs, and conical native American bark house*

*The author in front of some big redwoods, by no means the biggest*

I had a quick look at the Half Dome campsite which really didn't do anything for me. You could stay in a traditional looking tent structure, with poles and things but it cost $120 a night and it was packed full of tourists. No thanks.

So, I then looked around the Half Dome village, and at the Yosemite Valley Lodge, which looked really good but was a little bit pricey. I ended up at a place called Historic Big Trees Lodge at eleven o'clock at night!

I got a queen size bed for $70 a night. It was a beautiful colonial hotel that is 140 years old, in a really great location. The lodge was managed by the park rangers. They only had wi-fi in one room, which was cold!

I stayed for three nights there and used it as my base to get out and do day trips. The lodge was so big I couldn't fit it all in one photo!

The lodge used to be known as the Wawona Hotel, an equally historic name, until it was renamed on 1 March 2016. It was renamed because of a ridiculous-sounding legal dispute between the US National Parks Service and their former Yosemite concessionaires, a firm called Delaware North.

Delaware North had managed the park's facilities on behalf of the government for about twenty years before losing the contract to do so. In the meantime, it had trademarked many of the most famous names associated with the park, even the names of some geographical features it didn't manage, and was now in a legal dispute with the Parks Service which wanted its old names back to give to the new concessionaire.

It's quite common for such names to be trademarked these days, to stop some rip-off merchant putting them on a T-shirt without paying any royalties.

But somehow the parks service had been naïve or stupid enough to let Delaware North do the trademarking for it, and was now paying the price. Or rather, refusing to pay the price.

I have some printed maps and guides that have both the old and new names on them. These will be precious souvenirs for the future I think, especially if the Parks Service gets the old names back!

For more, see:

a-maverick.com/blog/yosemite-park-trouble-with-names

CHAPTER NINETEEN

# *Colorado: Cities in the Rockies*

AFTER Yosemite, I caught the train to Denver, Colorado. My intention was to spend four nights in Colorado. After that, I planned to catch a plane to Little Rock, Arkansas, which as you can see from the maps has no direct Amtrak rail connection to Denver. I wanted to look up former Arkansas Governor and later US President Bill Clinton's presidential library in Little Rock, after having read his autobiography. And I also thought it would be interesting to be there on election night, even though Hillary Clinton's election night HQ would actually be at the Javits Center in Manhattan.

I got my car at the Denver airport, which was an SUV, and I think the car knew how I felt about it. About five minutes after I picked the car up I did a U-turn and then they gave me another SUV. They had no station wagons – also known as wagons in the USA or estates in the UK – which was disappointing. Station wagons used to be as common in the USA as anywhere else, but they have almost been rendered extinct by the SUV craze. I just find SUVs too bloody big. Apart from that, the good thing about a station wagon is that you can sleep in it.

Throughout my travels I had met several people from Denver. One guy I met really ran the place down and really what he was saying would have put anyone off from going there, but not me. He was saying that they've decriminalised marijuana and thirty thousand deadbeats have gone to live there because of it. However, there are five other states that are meant to be decriminalising marijuana, and that will take the pressure off Denver when that happens.

We then talked about whether people were homeless in Denver because they've gone there for marijuana. I didn't know but I wanted to see it for myself anyway.

A pleasant city with a backdrop of the dusty blue Rocky Mountains, Denver is also the capital of the state of Colorado, the second most populous state in America's former Wild West after Arizona. Five and a half million people live in Colorado with nearly three million of them in Denver. In contrast, neighbouring Wyoming has little more than half a million inhabitants in the whole state, its largest city not much more than a farm town.

I'm not sure what Colorado's secret for encouraging people to come and live there has been – apart from scenery, of which there is no shortage in Wyoming either – but obviously it has worked.

Driving into Denver, I found that there was no car parking anywhere. On my first night, I stayed at the 11th Street Hostel. That was great. It had a fridge and a lounge in the room and cost about $33 a night.

I got talking with a guy there and I mentioned how I wanted to visit Boulder and Rocky Mountain National Park (which is singular by the way, not Rocky Mountains but Rocky Mountain).

He turned around and sneered, "those people at Boulder are a bunch of environmentalists who don't allow people to build and want nothing to do with oil – bunch of environmental snobs." I was a bit taken aback by such a negative description. I didn't tell him I didn't mind and that I was a supporter of environmentalists.

One thing he did tell me that was helpful was that the accommodation was incredibly expensive in Boulder: no doubt because the environmental snobs didn't allow people to build anything, assuming that was true. So, I stayed for one night in the city before heading off again. I did want to go to another national park. Winter was fast approaching, and I knew a lot of the roads would soon be shut and things like that, so I had to keep moving. I drove to a town called Estes Park and I got there on a Thursday afternoon. When I got to Estes Park, I drove a little further into nearby Rocky Mountain National Park and noticed that there were so many walks I could go on, that I thought the next day I would go back and do some.

I got a reasonably priced room in a place where I stayed for two nights. I asked the lady at the reception if it would it be the same price for both that night and the next. The lady at reception said yes.

Unfortunately, they didn't have a microwave in the room. Because I'm gluten intolerant, I have to make my own food a lot of the time.

The problem with some of the accommodation in the US is that it doesn't really cater for single people, I mean in my room there were two large double beds, I only needed a single. The price is reasonable for a family, but if you're a single person alone, you could spend up about $200 a day just on transport and hotels, and that would be skimping it.

So anyway, then, the next morning I asked about the room, and they said it was an extra $10. I didn't want to pay the new price of $87 just for me, and I was frustrated the price had changed overnight. I told them I wasn't paying that and that I would stay somewhere else. Then I realized I'd left my toilet bag there and I went back to look for it and it was gone, chucked out by the cleaners.

Then I thought blow it, I will try camping. So, I went and hired a sleeping bag and bought a water flask to take with me. I walked out the door with my sleeping bag but without the $22 flask, which I didn't realise until it was too late.

155

So, I was losing things all over the place – but I loved sleeping at the camping ground. I went to sleep looking at the stars. The bears were hibernating at last in these parts, so everyone was sleeping outside in tents, and to make things even better it was a very warm November for the Rocky Mountains. I was very lucky to be able to camp out.

I went back to the store after a couple of days out and told them about the flask. They said I lost the flask, but I don't recall taking it. I gave the sleeping bag back and went on my way.

To add to my troubles, I ran over my gas cooker and my gas bottle because I had to move my car in a hurry and simply forgot they were there. I decided I wasn't going to bother with a gas cooker anymore unless I could get a cheap one at Walmart.

Apart from all that, Estes Park was a lovely little town, and the locals were nice. When I went to the local store to get coffee there were people selling some crafts and things, so I bought a hippy bag and a wallet. I was a bit peeved though when they tried to charge me $19 when it clearly had a sign saying $12. I think tourist towns take advantage of you.

I went to the end of the road where all the trail heads ended, trails being what they call tracks in the US. I went to the Alberta Falls. Then, I went to an area called Mills Lake. Mills Lake was beautiful, and it was going to freeze over very soon, and when it freezes over it freezes with ripples in it, so you can't ice skate on it because it isn't flat. I thought that was interesting. The mountains looked amazing: they had glaciers on them.

It was in Mills Lake that I met a person called Colleen, and it was interesting talking with her about her point of view. Colleen was a Trump supporter. Something I noted was how people are so well versed in why they are voting for Trump. I spoke to her for a good couple of hours. She was a businesswoman, and her and her husband had been selling pumps for the last 20 years and they were based in Texas. It was really interesting getting the rundown from her. She said she disagreed with the US gaining open borders, and she talked about the costs of her small business, that they only had a 20% profit margin.

She said before Obama, they had what was known as Medicare, except now everybody calls the expanded system Obamacare. They pay healthcare for their employees, it used to be $6,000 a month and now it's $13,000 a month. She said that some of the regulations under President Obama were hard on them. She told me about one regulation which was that if their customers brought from them online, and then the customers' details get hacked, it becomes their fault for being insecure in addition to the criminal that's doing the hacking. Colleen did tell me that hacking is becoming a big problem there; but I think it is like that anywhere nowadays with the internet such a big part of our lives.

Colleen said she had stopped working in the company for the time being because they were waiting for the outcome of the election. If Clinton was elected, they were going to lay off two-thirds of their staff because they couldn't afford a tax that the Democrats had proposed.

She was a born-again Christian, but she was open to my views on religion. Colleen also said the reason why she moved to Colorado is because the standard of living in Texas was not good enough and that she was voting for Trump because she certainly didn't trust Clinton.

Colleen said she had initially supported Dr Ben Carson for the Republican nomination because he was a neurologist and a qualified individual. But he didn't get the nomination. She said that the Republican Party had withdrawn funding for Trump, so he had to put in his own funding; but then as the 'emailgate' charges against Clinton came to the fore, the National Committee had turned around and accepted Trump, belatedly. It was clear that support for Trump was far from universal among Republicans and was partly based on party loyalty alone.

*Fields of the red sandstone that gives the state its name (Colorado is a Spanish word for red, more poetic in its significance than Rojo)*

*Red Rocks Amphitheater, outside Denver.*
*Top: CC0 public domain image from Pixabay, by 'barrycdonovan'*

Colleen had health issues. So, she went trekking every day for exercise. She said you just had to enjoy each and every day for what it is. And I have to agree – I loved staying in my SUV under the stars. You have your bad days when you travel, and you will always get ripped off in tourist towns. But you have to enjoy each and every day for what it is.

Next stop was Boulder, the environmentalist town – maybe I'd fit in with my hippy bag. It was a one-hour drive there from Mills Lake

Boulder, Colorado, was a lot bigger than I thought it was going to be. I'd assumed it would be just a little place with a wooden sign saying Boulder, but it turned out to be a university city, whence its liberal reputation, with a population of 300,000. As the name suggests, Boulder is also a popular rock-climbing area, with excellent rock-climbing walls. There was red rock everywhere which was beautiful: I saw a lot when I went on a three-hour walk. The town was surrounded by parks, and I went to the beautiful outdoor Sunrise amphitheatre on Flagstaff Drive.

After that, I headed to Colorado Springs, south of Denver and a solid three-hour drive from Boulder.

The reason why I was going to Colorado Springs was because my father liked a true-life criminal TV series called Homicide Hunter that was set in Colorado Springs, in which a seen-it-all-and-then-some detective named Joe Kenda recounted some of his cases.

My father suggested I should go there and report back on what it was really like, so I did. I liked the town; the house prices were reasonable, and it did not seem overly populated even though it had a population of more than 700,000 people overall. Despite all those legends of the lonesome cowboy, about two-thirds of the population of Colorado live in and around Denver and the two neighbouring cities of Boulder to its north and Colorado Springs to its south.

There were plenty of pharmacies that sold medicinal marijuana, so I walked into one to see what that was like. There were about 500 different varieties of marijuana with their scientific name and a list of effects they could have on you. A guy offered to take me out to have a look at a marijuana farm, but I didn't go. I was surprised it was such a huge industry. I can't remember what the pharmacy was called: but it would have been Strawberry Fields, or Maggie's Farm, or the Healing Canna, or something of that sort: a far cry from the sort of pharmacy that is run by a conservative-looking individual in a white coat.

I ended up staying the night in Colorado Springs in the beast of a car I was driving.

Colorado Springs is more than a mile above sea level, but it was still warm enough for me to go around with casual jandals (or thongs) on my feet. I went on a railcar up to the top of nearby Pikes Peak, which is nearly as high as Mont Blanc and the highest peak that you can get to in North America by means of wheeled transportation, both rail and automobile. There is a tram to the top, an unexpectedly European touch, and also a road. All sorts of racers try scrambling to the top overland in buggies and dirt bikes, some of the latter with a special key connected to the rider's leathers so that when the rider falls off the engine cuts out. That's called American Hill-Climb. The idea is to get as far as possible up a really steep bluff on some sort of homemade special with big knobby tyres and a huge Harley-Davidson-type engine for extra uphill grunt, before falling off. A sort of dirt-bike rodeo in other words, more humane but even more crazy.

For me, it was a beautiful and relaxing ride up with a lot of history around it. I got to the top and there was snow, so I stood there in the alpine snows of oncoming winter with casual streetwear jandals on, which had seemed appropriate at the bottom. I went and dropped the SUV back at the airport that afternoon and then headed to the train station.

*Pikes Peak, at the top of the railway ride, with my streetwear standals!*

Still closer to Colorado Springs is Cheyenne Mountain, which has some more scenic attractions on top, but which is best known as the headquarters of North American Aerospace Defense Command (NORAD) between the mid-1960s and 2008. With its successive 25-ton blast doors in the tunnels that led down into a granite interior, tunnels that eventually widened out into caverns within which eleven multi-storey buildings sat mounted on springs, NORAD's Cheyenne Mountain HQ was designed to withstand an almost direct hit from just about anything. This was a fact that must have reassured the good folk of nearby Colorado Springs, living in wooden suburban houses, no end.

With election night approaching, I left for Little Rock as planned.

For more, see:

a-maverick.com/blog/colorado-cities-in-the-rockies

## CHAPTER TWENTY

# *Election Night in Little Rock*

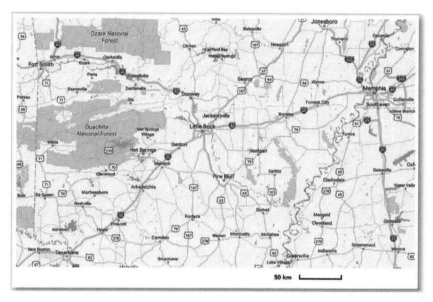

*Little Rock, Arkansas. Map data ©2017 Google.*

LITTLE Rock was where I was going to be for the election night. I wanted to sit in on the results as they came through to declare who would be the 45th President of the United States of America.

So, I did a search online about where I could go and sit in and watch it all unfold. It soon turned out that the local Democratic Party headquarters, of all places, weren't far from where I was staying.

This far into my travels, apart from my initial encounter with some Democrats in Houston, I had mostly met Trump-and-Republican supporters. I wanted to meet some more Democrats, so I emailed a woman called Sheila who was running things. She replied back and said she would be happy to have me join in. It was starting at 6.30 p.m., so that gave me time to go out for dinner.

Little Rock is the capital city of Arkansas, and was first settled by the French, who originally named it after a promontory called Le Petit Rocher – the little rock. It is a city that has grown to a metro area population of more than 700,000, and was once listed as one of America's most dangerous cities after a series of homicides in the 80's and then early 90's.

I found it to be a nice city with friendly people and I didn't let previous history taint my views. The city itself is quite small and sits on the banks of the Arkansas River. It is now one of the better American cities of its size to live in.

I spent the day in the city, looking around and I went to the William Jefferson Clinton Presidential Library, which was really impressive. It showed what Clinton, more commonly known as Bill, had managed to achieve throughout his Presidency. He appeared to have been a very talented President during his eight-year tenure from 1993 to 2001. There was the attempt at impeachment after his Monica Lewinsky affair, but the library did show he worked very hard for the average American. He was a great campaigner, too.

I arrived at 6.30 p.m. on the dot at the Little Rock Democratic headquarters, eager not to miss anything. I was greeted by Sheila. All up there were only about 100 people there. From all the reading I had done, I had understood that under the Electoral College system, it's not a direct vote.

The Electoral College is the group of people who make the final votes. Strictly speaking, those who cast their votes in the popular ballot are choosing their state's electors and not the president, although I'm not sure how many realise this.

*Little Rock overall, and Arkansas Governor's Mansion*
*(Top image is from Pixabay, CC0 public domain image by TheShiv76)*

The Electoral College system was developed partly to balance the votes out in geographical terms. In such a big country, larger states would always win with more people to vote for their states' candidates, whereas the Electoral College system allows smaller states more say. Each state gets two electors plus another elector for every seven hundred thousand people in its population, give or take a few. Thus, a state with well under a million inhabitants such as Alaska or Wyoming is three times more heavily represented, per head, than a state such as California or New York with tens of millions.

In 2016 the Electoral College was made up of 538 electors, and to be elected a candidate needed to have 270 or more of the Electoral College votes.

It's an interesting way to do things, anyway.

At the Democratic HQ the hype was irresistible, everyone was clapping and waiting for the first female president of the United States of America. The results were displayed on a big screen, and as they started rolling in, I began to see a bit of a pattern. The usual states that were known for being solid Democrat supporters, showed up as won by red – the Republican party and that meant Trump.

I could feel a shift in the atmosphere as the night went on. Florida was the biggest surprise to everyone, with gasps of shock as the colour for that state turned red too, then Wisconsin and Ohio. By 9.30 the winner was blatantly obvious, and people started to leave. It was obvious that everyone was in a state of shock: the predictions were all wrong. No one had expected it, it seemed.

Trump won.

That night, Hillary didn't concede defeat; people were in shock. She conceded the next day. It was a bit like Brexit: I don't think people imagined Trump could win. I phoned a few people back in New Zealand to tell them the news, and they were just as surprised.

I made my way back to where I was staying. I wasn't too sure what to think, really. Because as I said before, a lot of people I had met did support Trump.

I watched CNN and the country was angry. Hillary Clinton gave a very gracious concession speech and said you have you give Trump a chance, and then Barack Obama met with Donald Trump. Trump's main platform was to repeal Obamacare, but after meeting Obama he decided against this at least for people with pre-existing conditions and with regard to letting older children stay on their parents' insurance, a sensitive issue for teenagers. The following morning, I wasn't feeling the greatest, so I stayed in the hotel and turned on the TV again. You would almost think some extreme catastrophe had taken place. People were crying; and then the TV showed

that people had taken to the streets protesting, all over the country.

Trump was obviously a bit miffed by this and he sent a tweet saying they were professional protesters.

I hadn't realized that there were so many 'illegal aliens', to use Trump's own words – 'undocumented migrants' is more polite – who had been in America for a long time while the authorities had turned a blind eye, and were now very worried about being deported. People were genuinely very frightened. People were angry.

People were also angry because they were disenfranchised within the Democratic Party, where Bernie Sanders supporters were marginalized by the Democratic National Committee.

People saw a lot of their rights disappearing and they were obviously very frightened and/or angry about that. Even so, in Little Rock, 60.6% had voted Republican, and a lot of the places I had visited so far on this trip had been Republican strongholds. So, I really wasn't surprised.

In Portland and Seattle, they seemed to be angrier still. I sat and watched the protests and the TV reports and then documentaries all day, hoping the food poisoning I was once more suffering from would go away by the following day, as it did.

I went out to meet some locals and I met one woman who told me that she was sick and tired of the fact that the different races don't mix. I'm not sure whether she meant that from a liberal or a reactionary point of view, and I wondered if this would become more of a problem under Trump.

The next day I got a coupon deal for a massage. I arrived and was greeted by the owner, a white woman who had three children and a black husband. She told me that she went to Church, met her husband and then got married. She said that in Alabama they had a ball for blacks and a ball for whites, and her and her husband can go to neither of them. But I've been told that doesn't necessarily happen in Alabama, or not anymore. Anyhow she said that mixed marriages are quite common now and it wasn't really an issue.

Then I went to the hairdressers. The shop was called One Love and I thought it was closed. It was a hairdressing salon owned and operated by some black woman. They told me they could do my hair not right now but shortly, so I went out and had a coffee and came back.

I ended up being there for three hours talking with them. I had great conversation about business and life. The woman doing my hair was twenty-two. But she was already buying a house and was going to be a landlord. She was really onto it. I never saw any other white people come into the shop while I was there.

So, my stay in Little Rock ended up being very hospitable.

I woke early in the morning the following day, ready to hit the rails again. I wanted to leave my backpack in the railway station while I wandered around, but it was closed until 10 a.m.

The only place I knew close by was the restaurant I had been to on election night. The guy who served me was called Steven and he said I could leave my bag there until 5 p.m., which was nice of him. He mentioned he had seen me at the Democratic election night function, and he only remembered me because I had drunk orange juice all night. He asked where I was from. Then he told me he wanted to leave the USA and asked me a whole lot of questions about New Zealand.

He said that he just didn't want to live in an America that was ruled by someone who wasn't a decent human being. He just couldn't believe that his friends had voted for a President like that, who had put down women and different ethnicities, he said he just didn't feel he could be friends with them anymore. He said that Arkansas had voted for decriminalisation of marijuana, but at the same time didn't respect anyone else's freedom.

Steven said that when Trump came into power there would be some changes. He said his business wasn't doing so well, and he felt that because he was a known Democrat, he wouldn't get the work he wanted. He said he had worked for the Clintons before. So, he was seriously looking at going to New Zealand. Then he invited me out to dinner that night with him and his wife Brenda. I agreed and then headed off back into the city to explore, I had a whole day to kill.

I went down to the river walk and found some nice places to eat and have coffee. I met a lot of people there and had a really good time.

Steven and Brenda were lovely people and I enjoyed having dinner with them. I got the train later that night and, on the way back north, I ended up passing through a small town called Springfield where

Abraham Lincoln was from and was buried. I hadn't realised beforehand, or I might have got off the train for more than a few moments and had a proper look around.

St Louis, Missouri, including the famous stainless steel arch, top

Springfield, Illinois, including Abraham Lincoln impersonator, Bottom.

For more, see:

a-maverick.com/blog/election-night-in-little-rock

CHAPTER TWENTY-ONE

# Boston, Harvard, and the Big Dig

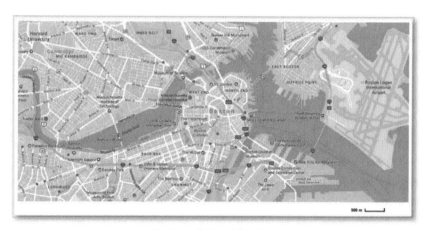

**Boston, Massachusetts**
*Map with north at top, above; Boston as seen looking westward, below.*
*Imagery and Map data ©2017 Google.*

FROM Chicago, I caught a train to Boston, Massachusetts. I was going to see the world-famous Harvard University. I also wanted to go to the Boston Tea Party Museum. I arrived in Boston on Tuesday night at 8 p.m. and I was to leave again on Thursday at 3 p.m. for Washington D.C. It was going to be a short, busy stay.

I got a hostel on Stewart Street. It was an outrageous $80 a night. I got there and saw smashed windows and speculated that it had been a bullet. I checked in because it was late, and I just wanted to go to sleep. They showed me my room, and, on the way, I saw another smashed window. It was shocking and very unpleasant.

So, I went up to the room and then decided to walk around and came across people talking about the sports rivalry between Boston and New York.

If you look on the internet, and you put Boston vs. New York, up pops an article about why Boston is so much better than New York, or vice versa. Apparently, there is even a 'city rivalry week'.

Particularly strong is the baseball rivalry between the New York Yankees and the Boston Red Sox, which has been going on for more than a hundred years and results in some heated conversations.

Anyway, after that rather horrific arrival, I decided I wasn't going out at night, even though the area I was in had a lot of theatre and movies which I'm sorry I didn't see. I decided the next day I wanted to go to Harvard and the Boston Tea Party Ships and Museum before leaving on the 3 p.m. train to New York. The Tea Party was, of course, the famous pre-revolutionary incident in which chests of tea were thrown over the side of British tea- ships by a band of colonists who had been careful to disguise themselves beforehand.

*Boston: Liberty Square, showing Hungarian Monument (top), Harvard University Law School Library in Langdell Hall by night (bottom)*

*Top image CC0 public domain on Pixabay by 'strecosa', architecturally rectified and slightly cropped for this book. Bottom image from Wikimedia Commons by 'Chensiyuan', CC-BY-SA 4.0, uploaded 14 November 2009; also architecturally rectified and slightly cropped for this book.*

On the waterfront, the Boston Tea Party Ships and Museum showed the origins of the War of Independence from the UK and King George III. The museum employed three actors to act like sailors and merchants on an old sailing ship, one of two actual eighteenth-century tea-ships, the *Eleanor* and the *Beaver*, which are tied up on the waterfront and form the 'ships' part of the museum complex.

*Liberal sentiments expressed on the*
*Harvard University campus*

Another really interesting thing about Boston is the way that a section of motorway on its downtown waterfront was placed underground recently, as part of a massive infrastructure realignment known informally as the Big Dig.

A park was laid on top. This is called the Rose Fitzgerald Kennedy Greenway, named after the mother of former President John F. Kennedy and his siblings. The Rose Fitzgerald Kennedy Greenway re-united the city with its waterfront and nicely complements the other inner-city parks, such as the Boston Common and Public Gardens, and the boulevard of Commonwealth Avenue behind

I got a cab to the train station, and it was only a four-hour ride to New York, which was good: no overnight sleep on the train this time!

For more, see:

| a-maverick.com/blog/boston-harvard-and-the-big-dig |
| --- |

## CHAPTER TWENTY- TWO

# *New York, New York*

*New York. Map data ©2017 Google.*

NEW YORK is the meeting place of the Atlantic Ocean and the Hudson River, and it is a city almost everyone has heard of.

Famed for its grand architecture and exuberant landmarks, New York is a place filled with excitement and an endless list of things to do. World famous places and landmarks like Central Park, the Empire State Building and the Statue of Liberty are found here.

I went on Airbnb and got a booking for $50 a night staying on a couch in Harlem. Harlem has become quite gentrified. Five years ago, you could get an apartment for $500 a month and that's now gone up to $1900 a month. The lovely young woman I stayed with was from the Dominican Republic and had been brought up in downtown Manhattan.

She had worked at Deloitte for three years and then chucked in her job, and now had no money to start up her own business. But renting out the lounge meant she could start putting money aside for that.

So, there I was in New York. I got Uber shared pooling and it only cost me $16. The Uber driver who picked me up was from Morocco but after five years he had become a naturalised American. Another two women using Uber were in the cab as well. They were from Kuwait and wore hijabs.

Anyway, we drove past the Trump Tower and the two women said, "boycott the Trump Tower." They said they had been here for a year and told me about why they had left Kuwait. I couldn't believe it, I did a quick Google search and in Kuwait you can't protest, let alone vote. They all said that they were Sunni Muslims, and they were surprised to find out that I knew what Sunni was. I said I had been to Pakistan.

I told them I wanted to go to Iran and see all the beautiful mosques and other buildings in places like Isfahan, and they said oh we wouldn't go to Iran because we are Sunni and Iran was Shi'a. I commiserated and said it was tragic that such divisions were so strong.

My plan was to spend Thursday, Friday, and Saturday night in Harlem, which is about a twenty-minute ride on the A train and about ten stops from Brooklyn.

In Harlem, it is quite safe to walk along the main streets at most hours, because people catch public transport until 2 or 3 in the morning. New York really is 'the city that never sleeps'. Or hardly ever. Certainly, even less so than London. And it is a real city that uses public transport till the same wee hours.

*Where I stayed in New York: not the Chelsea Hotel of rock'n'roll fame, but a place above the Chelsea Hair Salon!*

The buzzer didn't work at the Airbnb when I got there on 145th Street. I was lucky to have a mobile phone number to use. That would have been an issue with no key and no buzzer. Always get a mobile number.

I went to a jazz club called the Metropole Room on 22nd Street. There was a guy called John and his band playing. I got there at 9:30

p.m. and after watching him drink several glasses of wine one after the other, they played a few songs, and then finished after an hour.

I was surprised to learn that when your order a drink, you have to order two drinks minimum there. So, I had a yummy cheesecake and two cocktails which were reasonably priced at $11 each. Then they tried to get me to pay a mandatory tip for the band!

Afterwards there was a girl called Allie who was doing some Carpenters songs and some other jazz songs, which I really enjoyed.

On the Friday night, I went to a comedy club called Tribeca Comedy Lounge on 22 Warren Street. It was only $2. The comedians were great. I really enjoyed getting out and seeing New York culture on my first two nights.

I also explored the city during the daytime, including the famous beatnik quarter known as Greenwich Village, where a 1969 riot by drinkers in a gay bar called the Stonewall Inn, against police who were trying to arrest them for being that way, kicked off the modern gay liberation movement.

The Staten Island Ferry is free, and a good way to view the Statue of Liberty and the Manhattan skyline: the classic view. I also went on a boat tour that took me to Ellis Island, the famous immigration station that is now a museum.

I also went by ferry to Red Hook, an old manufacturing and warehouse district due south of Manhattan Island, with lots of old bring buildings and lofts and a generally run-down air. These days Red Hook has become an artists' colony. There are plans to extend the subway to Red Hook and build 45,000 apartments, which are needed, but I expect it won't be the same.

The new building on the World Trade Centre site was truly impressive. I'm glad something was rebuilt. Three buildings came down on that terrible day, incidentally, not just two.

*Harbour Ferry Tour, new One World Trade Centre*
*visible in photo below*

*Boat Tour, going past the Brooklyn Bridge (1883), Manhattan Municipal Building (1914) visible behind the bridge tower, New York City Housing Authority Alfred E. Smith Houses (1953) at right*

I don't know what to make of all the conspiracy and inside-job theories, the theories that the authorities knew what was going on but had somehow let it happen. Perhaps they had been keeping tabs on these individuals but simply hadn't realized what was about to happen – nobody would be very keen to own up to that!

## A Fickle Easter in Brooklyn

A bit over a year later, I decided to come back to New York and visit some people I'd got to know in the suburb of Red Hook, a waterfront district of Brooklyn. I had discovered the charms of Brooklyn and its waterfront enclave of Red Hook the year before. I had no time for the hysteria and street protests and wanted to go somewhere old-fashioned.

Brooklyn is just across the East River from Manhattan, via the Brooklyn Bridge – of course. There are also a few other bridges and and a tunnel to Brooklyn these days, but they aren't as famous as the Brooklyn Bridge, which was completed in 1883 and was significantly ahead of its time in engineering terms: the place where twentieth-century New York began.

Founded in the 1640s by the Dutch, not long after New York itself, Brooklyn is probably also New York's oldest suburb. It has a lot of charm.

Back at the time of the election, I had taken a boat-sightseeing tour of the harbour for the day and stopped at Fair Way Cafe, Red Hook. The food, the done-up wharf area, the brick buildings and the renewed warehouse area fascinated me, along with being so close to Manhattan and having a view of Lady Liberty.

*Manhattan and the Brooklyn Bridge*

*Brooklyn Heights street map*

*Graffiti Art*

*Brooklyn Street Scene*

Red Hook was the busiest freight port during the forties and fifties and was inhabited by seafarers from all over the world, even Norway.

*The Port at Red Hook*

I had scored a room in Airbnb at a reasonable rate in Coffey St, next to the murals depicting life in the area. My editor Chris Harris had begun corresponding with a writer from Red Hook called Russell Bittner and his partner Elinor Spielberg. By chance or cosmic concern they lived at a house across the way in Coffey Street as well.

Bike lanes are everywhere. They are so extensive you could bike to Manhattan, and many do.

*Bikes for Hire in Brooklyn*

When I first arrived the bus driver took a detour and said it was a shooting and went around Coffey St. It was a film shooting, an episode of *Law and Order,* and the set was guarded by the NYPD.

I received a random invite to a music evening called Woman of Color, featuring Ki and Sonic at a club called Nublu 151.

It was rap and great intimate music.

A weekly bus and underground pass is 32 dollars and the ferries from Ikea Red Hook are free during the weekends.

*'Detroit Police' car in Brooklyn!*

I got familiar with baseball – the Brooklyn Dodgers.

*The author and a Dodger*

I walked to the Brooklyn Historical Society and saw the sandstone ('brownstone') houses and churches. This area, which has now been urbanised for four hundred years, was one of the first to take up arms in the American War of Independence.

*Brownstone everyday architecture*

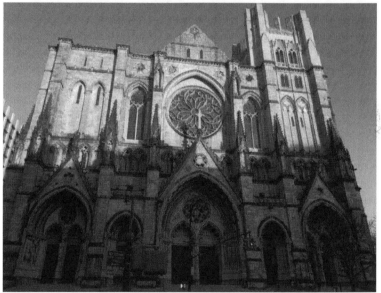

*Brownstone Churches*

The ferry being free, off I went wondering and wandering with my photography on the only fine and sunny day. I went to Central Park in

Manhattan and photographed all kinds of remarkable scenes, some of which I've reproduced in the next few photographs.

The next day it went from a comparatively warm 57 °F to snow. Wow!

And such was Easter!

For more, see:

a-maverick.com/blog/new-york-new-york

CHAPTER TWENTY-THREE

# *Washington D.C.*

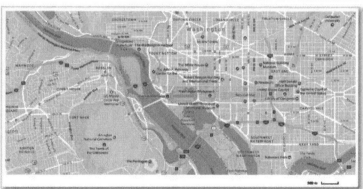

*Andrew Ellicott's influential 1792 revision of Pierre L'Enfant's original plan for the City of Washington (Wikimedia Commons, public domain); Washington today, reflecting the influence of the L'Enfant/Ellicott plan. Map data in present-day map ©2017 Google.*

FROM New York it was only another four-hour ride to the US capital city of Washington in the District of Columbia, spelt Washington D.C. for short.

I stayed in the Southwest district. I booked on Airbnb for $75 a night and hoped it would be better than the last one.

I arrived and there were plastic knives and forks in the kitchen, there was dog hair and dust on the carpet in the lounge. But at least my room was clean. They were subletting the room out illegally, but I ignored that.

The first day, I bused into the city with a $15 hop-on hop-off ticket that I'd purchased on Groupon and went sight-seeing. I got off in the front of the White House and walked around to take it all in. There are security guards around the White House, of course. You cannot drive around that area, but have to walk. I got photos of the garden that Michelle Obama started for school children.

I walked past the Dwight D. Eisenhower Executive Office Building, where I think I caught sight of Barack Obama. The security made everybody stop. We weren't allowed to cross the street, and he was followed by people on motorbikes.

The hop on, hop off bus was truly worthwhile. It was with Big Bus Tours, an authorized concessionaire of the National Park Service and the National Mall and Memorial Parks. They operate four colour-coded tours, the red loop on the National Mall, the blue loop past Arlington and other military sites, the yellow loop around the White House and Georgetown, and the green loop through the parks and past the National Cathedral, which is closed in winter.

I went to the Arlington National Cemetery, where John F. Kennedy and the early- 1900s President and later Chief Justice William Howard Taft are buried.

Seeing all the memorials and witnessing the changing of the guard in Arlington was amazing. It's a national shrine. There are thousands of soldiers buried there as well as various prominent state leaders, and it makes you aware of the sacrifice the US has made in various wars around the world and its own Civil War.

In Arlington, it was a profoundly humbling moment to be able to visit the gravesites of John and Jacqueline Kennedy (later, Onassis), which are marked by an eternal flame. John F. Kennedy was a President I admired. He was the 35th President of the United States, and made progress on a lot of good things before he was assassinated in 1963. The Arlington Cemetery had a lot to see, like the changing of the guard, the tomb of the Unknown Soldier and the Memorial Amphitheatre.

I went to the Lincoln Memorial, dedicated to the Civil War-era President who also fell to an assassin. The Lincoln memorial was the place where Martin Luther King gave his 'I have a dream' address, inscribed on the footsteps.

Then I went to an art museum and saw a painting of Abraham Lincoln, the 16th President of the United States. Apparently when he was standing for the presidency, he got a letter from an eleven-year-old girl named Grace Bedell, who told him that without a beard he wouldn't win the presidency. After being made President, he stopped in to see the child and thank her for her election-winning tip. I think that tells you what kind of person he was. I learned a lot at that museum, and it would turn out to be one of the highlights of my trip to D.C. I saw a photo of one group of black troops from the North who had volunteered to fight, and who all died in the war.

I wasn't even aware that the North had had an African American brigade. In fact, about 200,000 African Americans served in the Union Army and Navy: most were known at the time as US Colored Troops.

*The Lincoln Memorial*

My American civics education was proceeding by leaps and bounds. I soon discovered that Lincoln's first inaugural address (1861) is one of the classics of the English language: full of phrases that have become part of everyday speech such as 'the better angels of our nature'.

In the Lincoln Memorial, two shorter pieces were inscribed on the walls, the Gettysburg Address of 1863 and his second inaugural address of 1865. It was quite humbling to read these, too.

Then there was the Memorial to Thomas Jefferson. Jefferson, who came from Virginia, was the 3rd President of the United States. Before that, he was the main author of the Declaration of the Independence. He served as President from 1801 to 1809. The Jefferson Memorial also contains excerpts from Jefferson's writings on the walls.

The bus driver pointed out to me that Washington D.C. was right next door to Virginia, which is on the other side of the Potomac River. This led straight on to a few other interesting stories, including the origin of Arlington, which is not in D.C. but in Virginia, which went with the South in the American Civil War. Since Virginia went with the South, that meant that Washington was technically on the front line, though the Virginia side of the Potomac was soon occupied by the North and firmly defended for the duration. Arlington was the family estate of the South's most famous general, Robert E. Lee. The Northern occupiers turned Lee's fields into the famous cemetery; an unwelcome surprise for Lee when he came back from the war and discovered the full extent of the transformation, no doubt.

The bus stopped by the Washington Monument, close to where the District of Columbia War Memorial, a World War I memorial, stood. And also the memorial to US Civil War general and subsequent President, Ulysses S. Grant.

The National World War II Memorial has 56 pillars grouped around a plaza, pillars that symbolize the 48 states of the World War II-era USA, its seven federal territories and the District of Columbia; it was a beautiful memorial.

*Marine Corps and World War II Memorials*

Even though New Zealand later went anti-nuclear and effectively pulled out of its 1951 ANZUS defence alliance with the USA and Australia, the fact is that New Zealand and Australia both owed their relative freedom from invasion and attack in World War II to the American military effort in the Pacific.

The Vietnam Veterans Memorial bore the names of more than 58,000 American service personnel who died in that war, engraved into a black granite wall. I had seen a memorial to the same conflict in Vietnam some years before; I had now seen Vietnam memorials on both sides. I visited the memorial to the Korean War as well. This was organised around a platoon of stainless-steel statues of troops in ponchos, walking along in an imaginary rainstorm, with some photographs of those who fell eerily etched into another black granite wall.

We went past the Pentagon. The Pentagon was attacked on 9/11 so it was all guarded off. We just drove around all of those places. I could have walked around but travel does get tiring.

The capital city of the United States, Washington D.C. is a hive of monuments, museums, art and history. It's somewhere you want to go as a traveller at least once in a lifetime. There is no shortage of sights to visit, things to do and places to be in Washington D.C.

Geographically, the District of Columbia borders the states of both Virginia and Maryland, on the east coast on the United States.

The city of Washington was established as the permanent capital of the United States under the Residence Act of 1790. The Act stipulated that Philadelphia would remain the capital until 1800, to allow a reasonable interval for construction.

The famous city plan by Pierre l'Enfant was publicized in 1792, by which time the new capital had already been given the name of

Washington. The District of Columbia, as distinct from the city, was created somewhat later. The city was named in honour of George Washington, the very first President of the United States (1789-1797). Today, the American capital has a population of a bit over 600,000. But with people living outside the city that come there for work, the population goes up to around a million from Monday to Friday.

On a history roll, I visited the National Museum of the American Indian, which was shaped like a rock. The day I went they had a husband, wife and son team of dancers from the Squamish people of British Columbia in Canada, who were closely related to Chief Seattle's people on the other side of the modern-day frontier. They gave a fantastic one-hour performance.

The woman in the family group had done her PhD on native American culture and had choreographed the modern dances to ancient songs and wore beautiful clothing and outfits.

She talked about her son receiving his Squamish name when he turned 18 and how that had meant dancing and celebrations. She talked about how her ancestors had to leave their tribal lands and move to Alaska. The hardship that her ancestors had to endure meant that they did have a lot of benefits by comparison today, which she acknowledged. She also talked about the North Dakota pipeline and how water is a sacred right, so that everyone should be entitled to free clean drinking water. The way she put it was just so positive and I decided I just had to go to North Dakota to see the protesting. It was happening right at that moment on Standing Rock Reservation, and it was receiving international attention.

The museum had Native American food in the café which was really interesting and tasted amazing; I was truly impressed.

The National Museum of the American Indian is one of seventeen separate Smithsonian museums in Washington. The one most people probably think of as 'the Smithsonian' is the National Air and Space Museum (NASM), which displays the Spirit of St Louis in which Charles Lindbergh made the first solo flight of the Atlantic in 1927 and the Apollo 11 Command Module which once orbited the moon, among other remarkable items. But the NASM is just one of nineteen Smithsonian museums, in fact.

Of the other Smithsonian museums, their specialisms include aspects of African American life, natural history, American history, art, and other topics. There are seventeen Smithsonian museums in and around Washington D.C., as well as two more in New York. They are all named after benefactor Joseph Smithson, who died in 1829 and willed over half a million dollars, a considerable fortune in those days, to the US Government to establish an educational institute to be called the Smithsonian.

Remarkably enough, Smithson was an Englishman who never visited the United States. He died in Italy and was buried in Genoa. In 1904, his remains were transported to Washington D.C. and reinterred in a place of honour, amid great ceremony.

I made a booking to go to Capitol Hill on Monday morning. There was no way that I could actually get a visit to the White House as you need to book it three months in advance. This was disappointing, and well worth bearing in mind if you planning to visit the city yourself.

It was incredible to think that just a few years later the Capitol would be stormed by the rioters of January 6, 2021, looking for Vice President Mike Pence with more-or-less murderous intent while pretending at the same time to be tourists. A lot of people are calling for an inquiry to really get to the bottom of how this happened and who put the rioters, or "insurrectionists" as US Capitol Police officer Harry Dunn called them in his testimony, up to it. But, as of the time of writing, the Republican Party has so far blocked such an inquiry.

*The White House and the U.S. Capitol*

I met interesting people all the time here too. Many were very open to talking with me. Where I stayed in the Southwest there was a great supermarket – Target, where I could get healthy salads and other good food. I met a Nigerian woman at Target who worked in D.C. She moved there in 2004 to an apartment and was hoping to bring her family out, but her husband found another woman and her sister brought up her children. I think she finds life here expensive and quite hard.

I visited the remarkable Franklin Delano Roosevelt Memorial, more elaborate than an earlier, 1965 memorial that is just a block of granite with his name and dates on it. As with other monuments, the Franklin D. Roosevelt one includes quotes. I really agreed with this one: "The test of our progress is not whether we add more to the abundance of those who have much; it is whether we provide enough for those who have little."

FDR's wife, Eleanor, was distinguished in her own right, and became the first US ambassador to the United Nations.

The Martin Luther King Jr. memorial was also very moving. It is organized around a statue of Dr King emerging from stone, a statue which looks unfinished, as if Dr King's work is unfinished, the body only half free of the rock: which is probably the impression the sculptor desired to convey.

Washington really is the city of memorials and monuments.

The U. S. Capitol building was begun in 1800. It has 108 windows and there is a statue on top of it which represents freedom. The statue faces east, so that the sun never sets on the face of freedom.

There was a very interesting tale of how lobbyists came about. Apparently, President Grant used to drink whiskey in one of the local pubs and people used to go into the lobby to get his attention, and that is how the term lobbyist originated!

The tour went on. It turned out that the only woman to have a building named after her so far was Francis Perkins who was the first woman appointed to the US Cabinet, in the capacity of Secretary of Labor for twelve years under Franklin D. Roosevelt. Thus, the Francis Perkins Building contains the US Department of Labor today.

The White House was built between 1792 and 1800 and has 175 rooms, including 18 bathrooms. It is made of sandstone, which by tradition has always been painted white, and thus it is the White House.

Also impressive is the nearby Old Post Office, which Donald Trump renovated into a hotel before becoming President.

In a 2017 tweet, a former (2007–2013) Mexican ambassador, Arturo Sarukhan, accused the State Department of recommending the hotel to foreign dignitaries while Trump was President. Meanwhile, the Trump family has maintained a direct financial stake in the hotel. Earlier presidents would probably have sold out of the hotel if they had been in a similarly conflicted position.

For more, see:

a-maverick.com/blog/washington-dc

CHAPTER TWENTY-FOUR

# *Downtown Detroit: A City that is Becoming a Park*

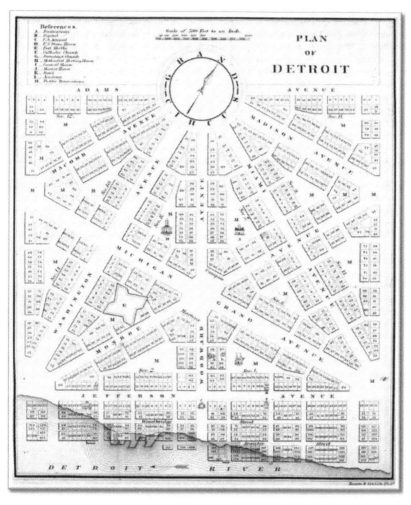

*Plan of Detroit (1806) by Augustus Brevoort Woodward, for reconstruction after the great fire of 1805. Public domain image.*

THE next place I visited was Detroit, in the state of Michigan. I had a friend there named Bill Chandler, the author of the guest history chapter with which this book begins, who had offered to show me around. Detroit was interesting. It is listed as a dangerous city to live in the US and has suffered massive depopulation since the 1950s. They call it the shrinking city. This expression is slightly misleading. It only refers to the City of Detroit, administratively and politically distinct from its outer suburbs, which are doing better.

In many American urban areas, the inner city is a separate local body from the suburbs. What often happens in these cases is that the older inner city falls into decay while the suburbs do nothing to help out. In the United States, ethnic prejudice and discrimination have played a large part factor in these trends, with the suburbs generally white and the inner city generally black. Black people were prevented from moving to the suburbs by various discriminatory means, and so the process of suburban development in the USA before and after World War II came to be dubbed 'white flight'.

Although black people had been present in Detroit from the time of the city's founding, the inner city became increasingly populated by a black workforce around the time of World War II. A major inner-city riot in 1967, caused by economic frustration and heavy-handed policing by a mostly white police force, has been blamed for the acceleration of the inner city's decline, though others say it was an excuse by which neglectful authorities have let themselves off the hook.

Many other cities have been turned around after inner city riots, which have often drawn attention to neglected problems such as police brutality and housing discrimination. But not Detroit. Downtown Detroit just kept on deteriorating.

Since the 1950s, the City of Detroit has indeed been in a downward spiral. The city has more than halved in population from a peak of 1.85 million, and its population is falling still. This is mainly because major car manufacturers who once made the city so famous have shifted production elsewhere. This is a huge problem of course, a bit like a mining town that's just had the mine close down. It helps to explain why Detroit's problems of inner city decline and suburban flight, though similar to those faced by many other American cities, are at the same time worse and more difficult to turn around.

It was a city of urban decay, which I saw for myself. Bill showed me around some of these areas, streets and streets of empty homes with boarded- up windows. It was like a ghost town. Locals talked about dead bodies inside the houses and homeless people taking over the empty suburbs. In 2015 Detroit City filed the largest municipal bankruptcy in the history of the United States. People had lost their jobs and their homes, and they were leaving on a massive scale.

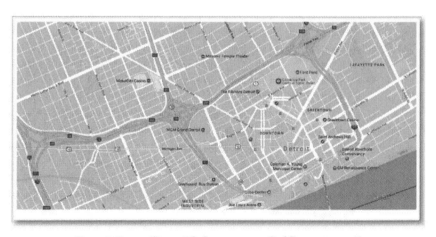

*Detroit Inner City, with freeways and older pattern of*
*radiating avenues based on the 1806 Woodward Plan*
*(Map data ©2017 Google)*

The black inner city was a thriving cultural area at first, so long as there were still plenty of jobs going. This was the era of the 'Motown' sound in the music industry, Motown being short for Motor Town: that is, Detroit. It was during this time that the council decided to build freeways, cutting through neighbourhoods and demolishing houses, churches, restaurants and more along the way. The freeways were paid for by the Federal Government; they wouldn't have been built if Detroit City had had to pay for them. The residents of the homes to be demolished were given just 30 days to vacate.

The 1967 riot was not the first. In fact, Detroit has the distinction of having been occupied by federal troops three times in the course of so-called race riots, in 1863, 1943 and 1967.

In the 1800s and in the first half of the twentieth century, such riots were generally started by the whites. They are probably best thought of as attempted lynchings or pogroms, in which the white mob found that in the big city the blacks could organize a defensive counter-mob more easily than they might have done in, say, rural Alabama.

These early race riots were not purely a question of whites versus blacks, either. It was more a question of White Anglo-Saxon Protestants ('WASPs'), initially the majority in many American cities and imbued with a sense of superiority, versus every other kind of ethnic group and every other religion. So, the Catholic Irish were also quite often the targets along with Catholics in general, Eastern Europeans, and Asians.

Such was the pattern of the 1863 riot, a white riot against the blacks more than a black one. The 1943 riot was also largely initiated by the white population of Detroit. Many local whites were resentful of the fact that 400,000 migrants, mostly black, had turned up in the region since the outbreak of World War II looking for war work that was well-paid in comparison to picking cotton in the Mississippi Delta.

In the 1943 riot no less than 34 people were killed, 25 of them black.

As I've suggested, the downtown could have been revitalized after the 1967 riot. Like Washington D.C. and Milwaukee, Detroit had 'good bones'. The city been developed on a plan in which grand avenues radiated out from an attractively planned city centre. On top of that, the inner city contained many stately buildings.

And the underlying social issues could all have been addressed, from poor relations between the police and the community to the ongoing changes in the industrial system and the financial fragmentation of the greater metropolis.

Instead, the focus remained on building freeways that strangled the city centre and accelerated its decline, while serving car-dependent suburbs outside the Detroit City limits. The city limits included the Eight Mile Road made famous in Eminem's 2002 movie *Eight Mile*. In the past, African Americans had been explicitly excluded from living in the outer suburbs. In the 1960s, the most explicitly racist policies of excluding black people from white-flight suburbs were dropped. But by this stage many inner-city blacks were becoming too poor to buy a suburban home, because the jobs were evaporating, too.

Thus, a beautiful and well-planned city was wrecked by a combination of inner-city freeways, de-industrialisation, and racism.

My train was an hour and a half late arriving in Detroit, so Bill picked me up at about nine in the morning. We didn't do too much for the rest of the day. We got a few things, and we talked about what we were going to do. We went out for dinner and then we visited another friend named Diane. It had been a day of sights and sights.

We began with a fry-up, which was good – I love beans with breakfast. Then we headed south on Lakeshore Drive, and Bill showed me a Cold War bomb shelter.

After that, we went to the Heidelberg Center where some burnt buildings had been cleared away. There isn't as much there as there used to be. Diane said that it was being dismantled.

*Michigan Mural by Ezra Winter in the lobby of the Guardian Building (1929). Like Miami, Detroit is a city with a lot of amazing Art Deco architecture.*

We went to Belle Isle, a parkland island in the river that is connected to the US mainland via a low multi-arch bridge erected in 1923. Belle Isle is larger than New York's Central Park and well worth a visit, like Detroit itself.

It was a beautiful day, clear and unseasonably warm. I liked the new condos going up at Rivertown, just east of downtown and close to Belle Isle. From here you can see the spectacular, Golden Gate-like Ambassador Bridge, with its long, high central span that allows ships to pass underneath.

The Ambassador Bridge links the USA to Canada and is the busiest single border crossing between the two nations. There are also road and rail tunnels under the Detroit River.

Back in the downtown, we visited the Michigan Soldiers' and Sailors Monument. We did the River Walk and visited the historic landing site of the French explorer Antoine de la Mothe Cadillac, the one who gave Detroit its name, détroit being French for 'strait'. We visited a monument to the Underground Railroad by which slaves had been helped to escape from the South, and Fort Poncho Historic Market. After that, we went back to the car and drove to the main post office.

I was shown the historic district of Corktown, the oldest remaining part of Detroit. Corktown was built in the Federal era of American architecture, known in Britain as the Regency period. This was a time of particularly dignified and restrained-looking architecture on both sides of the Atlantic, very plain when compared to later Victorian gingerbread styles.

Bill also showed me the impressive central railway station which entered service in 1914, but which is now derelict like so much else in Detroit; and then he brought me to my Hostel on Vermont and

Spruce. We got a little tour of the hostel and it turned out to be very spacious, clean and inviting. It was only $30 a night for a dorm room.

After that, we went to the West Canfield Historic District, which is another nineteenth-century suburb, and to Wayne State University. I was museumed out, so we returned to Belle Isle to eat banana and pumpernickel sandwiches.

It was about 3 p.m. and we went on a burned-out-house tour, the exact name of which I forget. Between Jefferson and Eight Mile, there is much urban decay: the business of touring it to view is called city porn by some people. The stretch between I-94 and Seven Mile was especially bad.

After that we cruised Eight Mile to a Coney Island restaurant. Coney Island is a chain in Michigan that sells hot dogs with minced meat in gravy on top, plus various other garnishes. Americans call this kind of hot dog a coney, after the New York amusement park of Coney Island.

I had a couple of coneys and some chili fries – 'mince and chips' as I like to call them.

We went back and chilled for a while and then decided to see the movie Loving which is about an interracial couple who won the landmark case in the Supreme Court Loving v Virginia, in which the Virginia state laws prohibiting inter-racial marriage were deemed to be unconstitutional.

Under the sinister-sounding Racial Integrity Act of 1924, which sounds like something the Nazis would have dreamed up, a mixed couple named Richard and Mildred Loving, Richard being white and Mildred part black and part native American, had each been sentenced to a year. The prison sentence was suspended on condition that they agreed to be exiled from Virginia for 25 years.

Unbelievably, this happened as late as 1959, with the US Supreme Court striking down the Racial Integrity Act and all similar bans on ethnically mixed marriage only as recently as 1967. Such laws had still applied throughout the whole of the Old South at that time and had indeed been in force in the majority of American states in the early 1950s, that is to say, even well after the defeat of the Nazis.

The movie was really good. It was understated, very well written and well-acted. The actors who played the appropriately named Loving couple were especially good.

*Detroit Industry Murals (1933) by Diego Rivera, Detroit Institute of Arts*

At ten the next morning Bill picked me up and we went to the public library so I could get some work done and he agreed to collect me again around lunch. I was feeling hungry by then, so we drove to get a snack, and then drove downtown and went to the Motown Museum. We were at the Detroit Institute of Arts a little after three. We saw the Diego Rivera murals and the famous Breughel wedding dance painting.

We had pasta for dinner that night, it was great to have a decent home cooked meal.

At 8:30 we were at Jerry and Mary's, friends of Bill's who he wanted me to meet. We talked about Detroit and the election. We were there a couple of hours and then I went back to the hostel.

Bill and Diane were both teachers. At one point while I was in Detroit, Diane mentioned how wages for teachers had declined in real terms since the 1990s, and the profession now lagged behind comparably skilled occupations even when benefits such as somewhat longer holidays were taken into account.

There is a lot of serious discussion among town planners and urban designers about how best to handle the depopulation of the inner city: whether communities should be consolidated into certain areas, while others are bulldozed and turned into parks, rather than letting the inner suburbs become full of vacant lots in a snaggle-toothed sort of a way. Detroit hasn't seen the last of urban renewal, it would seem.

After Detroit, we decided to see some more of Michigan. It was cool the next day, a cold, overcast semi-drizzly day when we set off. We were headed north via Flint, Michigan, another declining industrial town made famous in an early Mike Moore documentary, to the Straits of Mackinaw, the Upper Peninsula and the Canadian border at Sault Ste Marie, and then along the Lake Superior coast for a way, before returning down the west coast of the Lower Peninsula and back to Detroit.

We hit the road at ten-thirty. Our first stop on the intended circumnavigation of Michigan was a suburban McDonalds: we didn't get very far on the first leg of the expedition!

In the McDonalds, we talked to a lovely old man named Larry, who was hard of hearing. I wanted to talk about the water situation in the nearby Michigan city of Flint and Larry was more than happy to tell me about it. He had his hand on my shoulder when he talked, and he had some interesting things to say.

For more, see:

---

**a-maverick.com/blog/downtown-detroit-a-city-that-is-becoming-a-park**

---

# CHAPTER TWENTY-FIVE

## *Around Michigan*

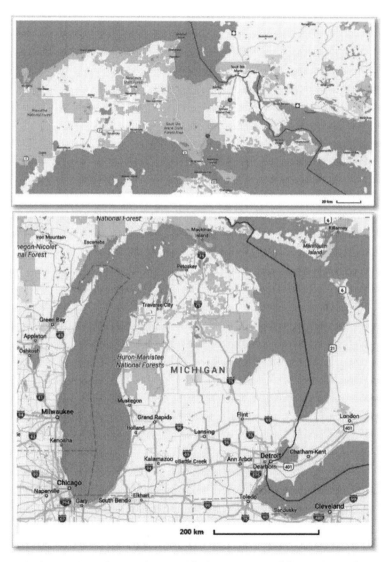

*Michigan: Upper Peninsula in the Mackinac Area, and Lower Peninsula*
*(Map data ©2017 Google)*

OUR next stop was Alabaster, where there is a historical market and an offshore landing facility for an old gypsum mine which no longer operates. It looks like a huge barn, floating on the water. I stopped an old couple in a pickup truck who told us about it; the people around here are really nice. We stopped at a small antique mall, and I bought a fake fur hat. We went through East Tawas and Oscoda and then we stopped at the

Sturgeon Point lighthouse. It was a short trek, and it was worth it.

We talked to a couple from Gregory, in the west of Livingston County, who were looking for Petoskey stones. Petoskey stones are a remarkable form of fossilized coral. When polished, they look like a turtle's shell, and they are the state stone of Michigan. These curious objects are called Petoskey stones because they were first found near a town named Petoskey. This sounds like an Eastern European name, but the town is actually named after a nineteenth-century Méti (part French, part Algonquian) fur trader and chief, whose Algonquian name was Pet-o-Sega.

Our next top was Presque Isle which, as the French name suggests, is not quite an island. The sky was just turning to dusk. There were two lighthouses, one from 1840 and one from 1870, it was quite beautiful. Michigan is girded by no less than 149 lighthouses. We got to another lighthouse just on dark, the Forty Mile Point Lighthouse – too dark to take pictures.

We pressed on to Mackinaw City at the northern tip of 'mainland' Michigan, known as the Lower Peninsula, at about 7 p.m. We checked into the appropriately named Lighthouse View Hotel. We had a good dinner at a restaurant called Audies, a couple of hundred metres from the Mackinac Bridge that spans the Mackinac Straits between the

Lower Peninsula and the part of Michigan known as the Upper Peninsula to its north.

Mackinac and Mackinaw are different spellings for the same thing, pronounced Mackinaw. The name is thought to come from an Algonquian word, mikinaak, meaning snapping turtle, and could mean 'many turtles'.

*Sturgeon Point Lighthouse; driving in the snow; Hiawatha National Forest: Bill's mother Nancy and her friend Ally with Mary Jane; near the Mackinac Straits, looking like it is time to put on the Mackinaw!*

The straits are windy, and so in English the word Mackinaw also refers to what we would call a freezer jacket in New Zealand: that is, a short jacket made from really tough, tight woollen fabric. With a woollen cap on top, the Mackinaw gives the classic Rust Belt working-man's look, like Robert de Niro in *The Deer Hunter*.

The Upper Peninsula is sandwiched between Lake Superior and Lakes Michigan and Huron. They are technically one lake because there is no change in water level along the Mackinac Straits. Lake Superior stands seven metres higher.

I ordered fish, which turned out nice.

We got up early the next morning and hit the road up to Sault Ste Marie, Michigan, at 7 a.m. This town stands on the St Mary River which flows between Lake Superior and Lake Huron. On the opposite shore was the larger town of Sault Ste Marie, Ontario, where we didn't go. The name means Saint Mary Rapids in old-fashioned French. In Michigan, at any rate, it is pronounced 'Soo Saint Marie'.

The rapids are at the Lake Superior entrance to the St Mary River. They are bypassed by the Soo Locks on the American side and by the Sault Ste Marie Canal, which also has a lock, on the Canadian side.

It was still dark when we stopped at a Nicky D's hamburger joint. Then we went to the park on Water Street where we saw the local landmark of the Indian Burial Mound. We also saw the reproduced stockade section of Fort Brady and the Fort Brady historical marker. Next, we drove a little east, and saw the SS *Valley Camp,* a bulk ore carrier launched in 1917 which is now a museum ship.

*Euphemistically-named conveniences
at Sault Ste Marie, Michigan*

There we saw a huge stone power plant from the early 20th century as well, and several historic houses side by side on Water Street. One had been inhabited by Douglass Houghton, a nineteenth-century geologist who first identified mineral ore bodies in the area. The other was the John Johnston House, named after an early settler, one of the first Europeans around. He was a loyalist during the American Revolution.

We left Sault St Marie behind and headed for the Big Bay Point Lighthouse on Lake Superior. We went west on route 28, filled up the car and then carried on. Sitting in the parking lot of Big Bay Point Lighthouse, I decided I need to start making arrangements to hire a car and drive to Standing Rock. Bill thought I was a little bit crazy.

There was already a light snow on the ground. On the way back, we were stopped on 28 by a state trooper, for doing 66 miles per hour in a 55 zone. The trooper looked like he could have been on a recruiting poster, chiselled jaw and all. He was nice and we got off with a warning – man were we lucky. Bill showed me some more of the countryside, which was beautiful. We stopped at a restaurant called White Tail in Brevort, just north of the Mackinac Bridge, which was excellent. I had bean soup and a bison burger and blackberry pie à la mode. We checked out old Mackinaw Lighthouse; then the snow started, and the roads were slick and dangerous. We stopped in at a café and thought we had better carry on because the snow was getting worse and we wanted to be sure of getting back to Detroit, and to be sure of meeting Bill's mother in Kalamazoo, Michigan, on the way. We carried on south along the western shores of the Lower Peninsula. Bill was going to show me some of the social contrasts in rural Michigan too, which after all that history I was very interested to see: the so-called twin cities of Benton Harbor and St. Joseph. The two are right next to each other but Benton Harbor is mostly, in fact overwhelmingly black and quite impoverished, while St Joseph is just as overwhelmingly white and much more prosperous. You can tell the difference between the two, stark contrasts really. More so because these towns are not very big, each with a population of about ten thousand, even though they are called cities.

I remember we talked a lot about class, what it means, and how we define it. According to a 2011 Michigan Radio article by Mercedes Mejia, called 'Bridging the Gap between Benton Harbor and St. Joseph', in Benton Harbor, forty-three percent of families lived below the poverty line while in St Joseph, it was six percent. And families in St Joseph, which the locals call St Joe, earned more than twice as much as their neighbours across the river.

We saw about fifteen cars that had skidded off the road. Taking it easy on the dodgy snowstorm highway, we sang songs and listened to Frank Sinatra on the way to Bill's mother's place. It took eight hours to do what should have been a four-hour drive as the snowstorm got even worse, and we didn't get in till a quarter to ten at night.

I got up at 9:30 am and found that Bill's mother, Nancy, was still in shock about the election result and couldn't quite get over the demise of the Democrats across three branches of government. She invited over her friend Ally, who was 75 and brought muffins.

Nancy had spent the last few years travelling the world, she had been to Vietnam, Cambodia and New Zealand. I had a look at her New Zealand photo album which had postcards and maps and fantastic photos of her travels. Ally talked about her life while we ate muffins, scrambled eggs, smoked fish and oatmeal bread (what a wonderful fry-up) and chatted for about two hours about potential race riots after the presidency. She stated her granddaughter, who was adopted from Ecuador, was frightened about Trump's presidency.

Then we drove back to Detroit and Bill kindly took me to the Amtrak railway station, and I picked up my tickets to leave. I was going to catch the train to the town of Minot in North Dakota, and then hire a car to get to Standing Rock, where the protests were being held against the Dakota Access Pipeline. I thanked Bill so much for showing me all over Detroit and taking me to meet his friends. It had been a great time and it was nice to see a familiar face, especially as Christmas was around the corner.

For more, see:

a-maverick.com/blog/around-michigan

## CHAPTER TWENTY-SIX

# Is Pure Water not a Human Right? From Minot to Standing Rock

CHINA is accused of crimes against the Uighurs. But what about Western crimes against indigenous people on their own land? Should we Westerners not be careful before casting too many stones? As we have seen, entire civilisations and very nearly entire peoples were wiped out by European colonisation.

But even in more recent times, a tendency to ride roughshod over indigenous rights continues. I was thinking of that, when I sat down to re-write this chapter about the long struggle between those who sought to build the Dakota Access Pipeline (DAPL) for liquid fuels, and the Atlantic Coast Pipeline for gas, through native American lands. The latter of these was cancelled in 2020 due to lack of proper environmental studies.

The DAPL was built and operated, but is the subject of lawsuits seeking its shutdown, driven by fear that it would leak and contaminate precious waterways and hinging once more on a lack of proper environmental studies.

I arrived in Minot, North Dakota, near the northern end of the DAPL pipeline route, for the second time at 9.30 a.m. It was really cold now, not just stormy, and the ground was almost knee-deep in snow. There had been a blizzard during the night, and I had to wait an hour for my taxi to arrive to collect me.

The taxi drove me through streets covered in sleet and sludgy grey snow that matched the sky.

The cab dropped me off at a local car yard, where I had arranged to pick up a rental. I collected the keys at the counter. But the people behind it didn't want to come out of their warm office and show me where the oversized pickup truck they had given me was, let alone the finer points of how to drive it.

*The Dakota Access Pipeline (red) and Standing Rock Reservation (orange) by 'NiftyG', 3 November 2016, CC BY-SA 4.0. via Wikimedia Commons, The pipeline originates in North Dakota, at top left, and flows to Illinois, at bottom right.*

Trudging alone through the snow with all my bags, I found that all the number plates had been covered by the latest dump. I couldn't tell which truck was mine!

It was twenty-seven degrees below zero on the Celsius scale, so cold I had to be wary of frostbite on my face and fingers and could hardly breathe. I had to find the truck soon and get its heater going. Finally, I discovered it: a big red Toyota.

Breathless, I got in and started the engine. I was more than a bit nervous about driving such a behemoth in the evidently appalling conditions of a North Dakota winter.

I found a nearby hotel on my device and drove there to book in for the night, and then practiced driving the truck all the rest of the day! The next morning, I left for a city named Bismarck, which was a hundred miles to the south.

Bismarck is the capital of North Dakota. It has a population of 61,000 and is about sixty miles by road from the town of Fort Yates, the tribal headquarters of the Standing Rock Sioux. Along with its Native American heritage, North Dakota has interesting German and Norwegian beginnings, whence the name of its capital city.

I went shopping immediately and got a whole lot of stuff like snow boots and things. I had to do it quickly because I had read an article on the train where the chief of the Standing Rock Sioux, Dave Archambault II, who was more formally known as their Chairman, had asked all the protesters to leave Standing Rock, their work done supposedly, after the Army Corps of Engineers denied a permit to drill under the Missouri River and Lake Oahe, a long, thin lake formed by a dam on the Missouri that forms the eastern boundary of the Standing Rock Sioux Reservation and the Cheyenne Reservation to its south.

I felt I might miss it all. But the protesters did not want to leave. My idea was to stay at the local tribal-run casino and try and talk to the people who have spoken to the media already.

A guy I had met on the train told me not to tell anyone that I was going to Standing Rock. I wasn't sure why, and it made me a little uneasy.

## A Dakota Pipeline's Last Stand

The protesters in North Dakota were making a stand against an oil pipeline being built through Standing Rock Reservation on Sioux tribal lands. It was not just the Sioux people there either, it was people from all over: other Native American tribes, environmentalists, US celebrities and even New Zealanders and other international people.

The Dakota Access Pipeline (DAPL) project was a scheme that was to see a 1,170-mile-long oil pipe built underground, but also running below and across waterways like Lake Oahe.

The pipeline was seen as a cheap way of sending oil across the country. With the price of oil in decline, jobs in the industry were becoming fewer and people were leaving Minot. Many hoped that the pipeline would turn things around.

Unfortunately, there has been no shortage of leaks and oil spills with these types of pipelines, and it puts the land and water under threat.

The police and federal government agencies had turned up and fired rubber bullets and water cannons on the protesters even in the freezing temperatures. I found a number of harrowing videos that had been released online from the camp where that was happening.

The pipeline, also known as the Bakken Pipeline, was proposed to run from North Dakota's Bakken oilfield, transporting 570,000 barrels of oil every day. It was to cross a number of waterways, 200 in fact, any of which might have been in danger if there was ever a leak or spillage: and there would be, if the history of other pipelines around the US was anything to go by.

The Sioux tribe or Great Sioux Nation is broken into three distinct groups, the Lakota, Dakota and Nakota tribes. Their tribal lands once made up a good part of the states of North Dakota and South Dakota and some other areas, but over time have become segregated scatterings.

So, I could understand their need to protect their land and their waterways and drinking water. It is not just an American problem but a global one. I have seen it in New Zealand as well.

## Driving out to the Camp

Getting to Standing Rock turned out to be one of those things where you're in the right place at the right time.

I got talking to a guy called Jeff – not his real name – in the library in Bismarck. It turned out that Jeff was one of the front-line warriors in the protest, and he offered to take me to one of the camps involved with Standing Rock Reservation where he and a few others were camped out in support of the "No DAPL Pipeline" protest: a protest that was given international attention even as far away as New Zealand.

I asked if I could interview him, and he agreed.

First, I asked where he came from, and what Native American tribe he belonged to. Jeff looked at me with his dark eyes and began his story.

"I'm from Leech Lake Minnesota, I'm Anishinaabeg, I live in Minneapolis now, and then we have the KXL pipeline that we have been fighting for about five years now, and we still haven't beat it, but we did get some victories with that so…"

"So, who's putting in your pipeline?" I asked, and he replied, "KXL" [Keystone XL]. I asked him who KXL was.

*Jeff in the passenger seat; Standing Rock; Dakota roadside conditions*

Jeff paused for a brief moment before continuing. "I'm not sure, I'm not exactly sure. I mean it's all tied to the same; they all have different like Energy Transfer, like different names. But it's all, they are all tied to like, Enbridge is the one in Minnesota. So yeah, the Enbridge one is the one we are fighting, the funders ended up pulling their money out of that pipeline, so it's not defeated yet but it's a big step that the funders took their money out, but what they did is put that

238

into the DAPL pipeline. So, I guess that's why a lot of me and my people felt obligated – you can't just put your problems off on the next state, you know? So that's why we came here to try to help people in any way that we could. Yeah, been here for four months".

I laughed a little at that and I said, "So you originally only came for four days?

"Yeah, we came for four/five days and then it just ends up it is hard to leave. I left for three days, and I was just itching the whole time to come back so I came back, and I have been living here since."

I had skidded a few times in the snow while driving in Minot and had even gone through a red light quite unintentionally as a result. But the country roads seemed to be safer as the snowploughs cleared them regularly. Around town, there seemed to be more snow.

## At Standing Rock Reservation

It's a fight over pure drinking water – a human right. This is for all communities worldwide. You can see the fight in Nepal between China and India over water. I recently bore witness to that. So, water is the new gold.

I did not use a press pass, nor did I interview Chairman Archambault or another Sioux leader named LaDonna Tamakawastewin Allard, who sadly died in 2021: both respected leaders to their own followers, who had received interviews on social media. I received their Twitter messages.

The pipeline company, DAPL, has a record of around 80 spills in 20 years, the latest being the same month and year as the protests, December 2016 and it was no wonder they were worried. You'd think that'd make the DAPL owners worried, right?

When I was at Standing Rock, I took photos for two minutes and then I had to sit in the car and put the heater on, and it took me ten minutes to heat my hands up.

*Standing Rock, 27 °C below*

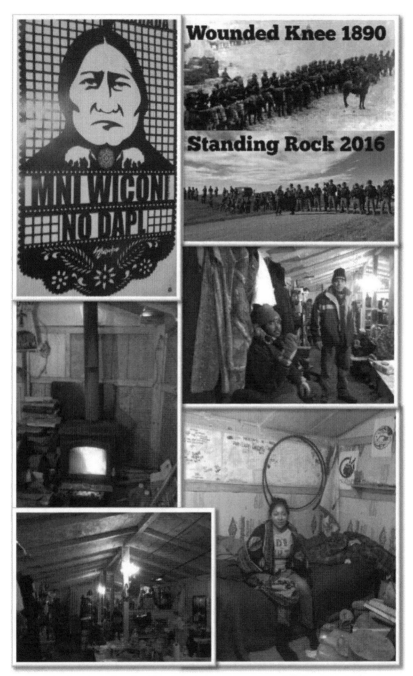

*At the Standing Rock protest camp; protest publicity material*

There was a blizzard coming and the camps at Standing Rock were not prepared. Sleeping bags and tents made for snow are specialist equipment.

The only people to survive or remain long term needed permanent structures or specialist tents with heating: with propane, teepees are ideal for the conditions. There were quite a few teepees erected at Standing Rock. Eight thousand people had gathered and there were lots of camps with different philosophies like the ones Jeff mentioned: Red Camp, Rosebud and Satellite. All meals were provided and sometimes accommodation. Screening people had become a necessity also.

By now, the police had closed the road down which Jeff and I had come, and some of the others as well.

I decided the gods must be looking after me. I know that a crew from the Māori Television current affairs programme Native Affairs had been to Standing Rock. But I was not part of a film crew with a driver, a photographer, a writer and full accreditation. I was just there from New Zealand by myself.

Jeff introduced me to his new family, Sasha Beaulieu, and Chad who was recovering from being tear gassed. It had badly affected his lungs. Jeff said his new family at Standing Rock meant everything to him, he gave up his job and home to make this last stand. Sasha said she was not part of the United States as her tribe had not signed a treaty.

An ancient cleansing ceremony had been conducted – Chad had started chanting. I felt like an intruder, but after all I was Scottish, and we knew all about dispossession and playing second fiddle to the English.

Sasha and I had connected immediately, and I promised to send her a dictaphone so she could write her story. I gave a food donation, and they said I could stay but they urgently needed wood as another storm had been forecast for the next day.

I met Dili from British Columbia, who was leaving as her car had been stuck and she was not prepared. People had just dumped tents and gone. Jeff and his crew were clearing up, they were all thankful for Jeff being there. I in turn, was thankful to have the opportunity to meet them. They asked me if I would like to stay and if I wanted food, and I said I would help in other ways. I stayed three hours all up and we discussed many things.

The Chairman had indicated that he had made a mistake asking all those to leave. There seemed to be a bit of distrust. Jeff and the frontline warriors had been of the view that the pipeline would continue, and there had been reports that the drilling hasn't stopped, even though there had been an Obama Federal decision, and that Trump was going to overturn it when he was inaugurated on January 20th.

Why did Obama not do more? Justin Trudeau soon gave in to the British-Columbia pipeline up in Canada. Corporates, it seems, dominate and humanity is doomed if we cannot stop this polluting madness. I agree with Chad and Jeff. It is common sense that humanity has pure drinking water.

For more, see:

a-maverick.com/blog/is-pure-water-not-a-human-right-from-minot-to-standing-rock

CHAPTER TWENTY-SEVEN

## *Charlotte: the most boring town in America? Billy Graham and car racing, not for me*

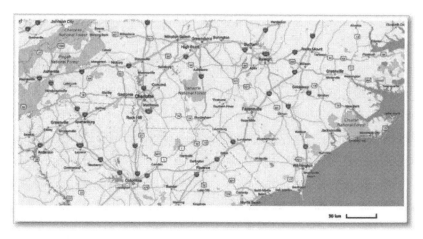

*Charlotte, regional map and view of downtown looking northward*
*(Imagery and Map data ©2017 Google)*

$A$FTER Standing Rock, I was ready to tackle more social movement issues, so I got a train back to Chicago once more, stayed for a night and then headed south. Way down south by plane this time. It was only 2 hours by plane rather than about 20 by train.

I flew into Charlotte in the afternoon: the largest city in the state of North Carolina. In 1761, when the thirteen colonies were still British, the infant city was named after the wife of King George III, Charlotte of Mecklenburg-Strelitz; the same royal person that Queen Charlotte Sound in New Zealand is named after.

I found Charlotte to be an overly sport-focused city, with a 'jock culture' as the Americans say.

According to a recent entry on Wikipedia, "Among Charlotte's many notable attractions, some of the most popular include the Carolina Panthers of the National Football League (NFL), the Charlotte Hornets of the National Basketball Association (NBA), the Charlotte Independence of the United Soccer League (USL), two NASCAR Sprint Cup races and the NASCAR All-Star Race, the Wells Fargo Championship, the NASCAR Hall of Fame, the Charlotte Ballet. Carowinds amusement park, and the U.S. National Whitewater Center."

Well, at least they have a ballet. I stayed for two nights there and the whole time all I could think was what a boring place. There was nothing there that interested me, it was all cars and car racing and jock stuff, or pretty nearly so.

The most interesting thing I learned about Charlotte was that it was once occupied by the Catawba Native American Tribe and that in 1759 there were 10,000 of the Catawba living in the Charlotte area. In 1826 there were only 110. It's crazy to think that contact with white people caused that population crash, mostly as a result of smallpox and other diseases.

*Charlotte, downtown.* Pixabay public domain image by 'carissarogers'.

Actually, I did one cultural thing while in Charlotte and that was to visit the Billy Graham Library. I convinced myself that there had to be something good about this place to set against the dreadful deaths of virtually an entire Native American people.

Billy Graham was an evangelist who revived a charismatic form of Christianity in the USA and across the world. He was quite a popular person: in 2007, three former presidents – Jimmy Carter, George H. W. Bush and Bill Clinton – attended the opening, in Charlotte, of the library named after him.

*The Billy Graham Library (the premises are designed to look like a farm),*
Wikimedia Commons image dated 12 July 2012 by Billy Hathorn, CC-BY-SA 3.0.

Billy Graham was one of the first southern preachers to openly oppose segregation in the early 1950s, and often went on the road with the legendary civil rights activist Dr Martin Luther King, Jr., better known as just plain Martin Luther King.

But apart from that, I felt like I yawned my way through almost two days in that city. Sorry Charlotte but you take the number one spot for the most boring city I have ever visited in America.

One of Charlotte's big problems in terms of acquiring more snap is that its downtown area, tightly circumscribed by a motorway bullring, seems overly devoted to open-air car parks and sports stadiums of various sorts. Both are notorious killers of city life and belong outside the motorway bullring, not inside. Also inside the bullring is the

NASCAR Hall of Fame, a car-racing museum. Again, that's not the sort of thing that belongs in the absolute centre of town.

This is what happens when you have too much input from the jocks: sports-mad types I mean, not the Scots (we see it in New Zealand, too).

The only way to make the city centre come alive is to encourage the sorts of things that go with walking around and hopping on trams: pretty much the opposite of team sports, and of car culture as well.

The failure of Charlotte's downtown is made worse by the fact that Charlotte has less than half the population of Houston in its hugely sprawling metropolitan area.

Houston developed in a similarly car-dependent manner; but so many people live there these days that it has developed a lively downtown anyway, complete with an eventually revived tramway. There's something for everyone in Houston. But a city like Charlotte has to work harder to keep the sparks of the life downtown from going out, and not pour cold water on whatever remain with yet more stadiums, carparks, and motor museums.

I was excited to head to Alabama. The train was going to leave at 3 a.m., which was just not ideal, so I decided I would drive. I hired another rental car, this time with much better service then in Minot (the snow wasn't hiding things in Charlotte, of course) and drove for six hours through the countryside to old Alabammy.

For more, see:

a-maverick.com/blog/charlotte-the-most-boring-town-in-america-billy-graham-and-car-racing-not-for-me

CHAPTER TWENTY-EIGHT

# Birmingham, Alabama: A much more interesting city

ALABAMA sits in the southeast of the United States. The population of the state is roughly five million and the biggest city in the state is its capital city, is Birmingham. It is a place filled with very recent civil rights history and an iconic place to visit for those interested in that. I mean, I only have to mention the name of Dr Martin Luther King Jr – that says it all.

I stayed in a place that cost $74 a night. It was horrific: the roof leaked and the tiles in the hallways were wet, so you had to be careful you didn't slip over.

I went out into the city and looked around and met a few people. One woman I spoke to told me she prayed every day. Her husband was a cop and had two sons. We talked about the old civil rights protest days, and she surprised me by saying, "you know they had to put the dogs on the children because they wouldn't stop what they were told to do". She said, "if a cop, if a policeman tells you to do something you do it". I thought well not necessarily, not when it comes to protesting, because the state of Alabama had opposed the Federal Government, segregation was meant to be ending but it didn't, so people protested.

There was a huge civil rights movement in Alabama in the 1950s, started by Rosa Parks and her Montgomery Bus Boycott. Rosa Parks was arrested for refusing to give up her bus seat for a someone who was white on a bus in the smaller Alabama city of Montgomery, so a yearlong boycott of the bus system began. It hurt the bus companies because 75% of the passengers were black people, and it got their attention. In 1956 the Supreme Court ruled it was unconstitutional for public transport to be segregated.

(In later years, buses were also used to mix up school pupils from majority-black and majority-white neighbourhoods by federal decree so that they would attend the same classes in school, a policy called 'busing'. It is interesting to note that interesting to note that in the 1970s Joe Biden was opposed to this further extension of integration.)

In 1960 Birmingham was still one of the most divided cities, in terms of black vs white. Students from the Birmingham University were part of the protest the woman was referring to. The police used dogs on children and the students who were part of the protest. People went out and protested nonviolently and in civilly disobedient ways – so they didn't listen to the policemen telling them to go home. These protests helped give rise to the 1964 Civil Rights Act: meaning no one should be discriminated for in anything simply because of their colour.

Especially interesting for me was a downtown museum and interpretive centre called the Birmingham Civil Rights Institute, or BCRI for short. There, I learned that a local commander had arrested so many people that they had to use schools to keep people in.

Birmingham was one of the biggest industrial cities in the south. Back in 1960 the population was 720,000, of which 240,000 were black. It is really interesting how the policies of South African apartheid and American segregation were almost identical, in terms of buses, housing, etc. After blacks got the vote at the end of the Civil War and for a time played an active role in politics, the black vote was gradually suppressed by means of various tricks such as poll taxes and property taxes, as well as the outright terrorism of the Ku Klux Klan.

In Alabama, many black people were disenfranchised well into the sixties. This was a policy that the Civil Rights Act confronted head-on, though voter suppression continues to this day by means of policies linked to the criminal justice system, such as denying ex-prisoners the right to vote: policies Michelle Harrison calls The New Jim Crow in her book of that title, after the nickname for the old systems of suppression of black civil rights. In Alabama, they just simply refused to follow the anti-racism statutes that were eventually enacted at the federal level, where racist movements like the Klan had ultimately failed to take over. They said it was a state matter. Dr King was arrested and locked up in a Birmingham city jail, where he wrote a famous letter of protest.

There were the so-called freedom riders, busloads of students and activists down from the north: they were dragged out and beaten up and some even murdered. It looked like it was extremely hateful, and it wasn't actually that long ago.

From the BCRI I crossed 16th Street to Kelly Ingram Park, where important protests had happened in the past and which was now full of powerful sculptures on civil rights themes.

This part of town is now designated as the Birmingham Civil Rights District and was also proclaimed as the Birmingham Civil Rights National Monument by President Barack Obama in 2017.

The Civil Rights District includes the Sixteenth Street Baptist Church, just across 6th Avenue North from Kelly Ingram Park and the BCRI. I was amazed to hear that this church had been bombed by Ku Klux Klan members on a Sunday in 1963, a hate-crime that killed four young girls and injured a larger number of other worshippers, generally stated as between fourteen and twenty-two. I made a note to watch the Spike Lee documentary *4 Little Girls*.

Even after all that, the Klan still had the audacity to pop up in Birmingham the day after Trump was elected, leaving fliers on car windshields this time.

More recently, some Confederate monuments have been taken down in Birmingham and other Alabama cities, with the mayor of Birmingham, Randall Woodfin, opting for his city to pay a fine under the Alabama Memorial Preservation Act after tearing down one of the monuments in 2020, rather than risk further civil unrest in the aftermath of the killing of George Floyd and other such high-Black Lives Matter cases by not tearing it down.

I also visited the Iron and Steel Museum of Alabama at McCalla, in the suburbs of Birmingham. Birmingham stands on vast reservoirs of iron ore, which give their name to the Red Mountains just outside the city. At the time of the American Civil War, Birmingham did not yet exist, and the iron ore reserves of Alabama were largely untapped, the Southern slavers preferring to grow cotton instead.

You might recall that scene in *Gone with the Wind* where Rhett Butler chides his fellow Southerners for proposing to go to war against the North without a single cannon factory to their name. The Confederates had some iron works but not anything comparable to the North. Which is one reason why they lost.

Birmingham, which was supposed to be the cradle of a new and more industrial South, was founded in 1871. It was named after Birmingham, England, at that time the most important industrial city in the UK. There were Polish and Lebanese people who worked there, immigrants from all over the world, plus the Scottish and the English.

In truth, I loved Birmingham. I walked into a hippie store in the Five Ways district of inner-city Birmingham; and that's where they had all the restaurants as well. I went to a place called Golden Temple health, foods and vegetarian café: they had some great meals there.

*Entering Alabama; Birmingham Museum of Art*
Lower image CC-BY-3.0, Seth Pathasema, Birmingham Museum of Art

*Birminham Civil Rights Institute dome and steps (source: US National Park Service); Statue of the Reverend Dr Martin Luther King Jr ,and the statue of the Three Kneeling Ministers, both in Kelly Ingram Park*

I met and interviewed a woman named Judy, who went to Kelly Ingram Park every Friday out of respect for what had happened. She believed that white people need to show that black lives do matter.

Judy introduced me to her friends Sherry and Winnie. All three were white women, and they happily volunteered to talk with me about an organisation they had just founded, called White Birminghamians for Black Lives. I wanted to find out more and they readily agreed to speak with me. I hit the record button on my phone and began with the question, "So tell me, why did you start the movement?"

"The name of the action is 'White Birminghamians for Black Lives'," Judy told me, "and we started it on September the 23rd. It was the week of the police shooting of Mr Crutcher in Tulsa, and Mr Scott in Charlotte in North Carolina. And I just felt that I had to get out of the house and show some opposition to the rash of police shootings, it's been a rash of them, but they have been going on for decades. And so, I posted an event on Facebook and we had the first witness that afternoon, and we have continued them on Fridays since then. And the point is to particularly invite white people who have a conscience to oppose violence and discrimination against people of colour, to come out and make that statement – to have a place that they know that they will feel welcome and that they will be given something constructive to do. And it's for everyone who feels that white people need to stand up for racial justice."

"Ok and have you just got one organisation here or has it grown into a national organisation?," I asked, interested and completely absorbed by the three women who had volunteered to talk with me.

"Well, we are not an organisation and don't have any ambitions to be that" said Judy, gesturing with her hands, "we are simply a series of activities that take place in this park on Fridays. But we work closely with the local Black Lives Matter chapter – there is a Black Lives Matter Birmingham chapter, and there is about to be a local chapter of 'showing up for racial justice', a chapter of the national group, that particularly organises among white people, in conjunction with Black Lives Matter. And we are in touch with a number of other good things that are going on within the city – that's one thing that we do is, help people know what all is going on and how, if they come to a witness here, they can learn about other things they can do in an organisational way about social justice and other issues."

I hit on some serious issues: "I've seen a recent documentary about the rise of the Ku Klux Clan and also there was a Ku Klux Klan march in North Carolina in the third of December – and that occurring had been released by the black member – I have forgotten her name, I'm not good with names, on the Democratic National Committee. Do you think that more white people are going to have to stand up and show that they believe black lives matter, considering the rise of the Ku Klux Klan?"

"Well, I think it is a dangerous time in our country," Judy said forthrightly, while Sherry and Winnie nodded in agreement, "I think the politics of the recent Presidential campaign have emboldened a lot of the old prejudices and fears, that have never died away, and that we have never dealt with adequately. And so that is one thing that we are doing is casting a wide net and inviting all people of good conscience to come out and tell the truth about themselves, which is that at heart we want a real democracy, and we want equality for everybody in the nation, so it is a time of danger for our democracy. And there are negative voices that are empowered, but that just means that it's a time where people of good will have to be more visible and more vocal than ever and cannot lose hope."

"Yeah, it's very cynical that divide and conquer has worked so beautifully and so manipulatively," Sherry added. "You know, appealing to the worst in people – let's blame the immigrants not our government that has really failed us, in terms of some of the crises that we have gone through."

"Very interesting," I said, "because I just went and visited a local shopping centre. I went and bought food for a friend of mine who I'm going to send to Detroit, and I said everyone says why did you want to come to Birmingham, and I said 'Well, Birmingham seems a lot more interesting than Charlotte!' "And the women there turned around and said, 'What is there to see here?', and I said, 'Well you know you have got a history of civil unrest and so on'."

It's amazing that the segregationists here were so stubborn. The President had to personally intervene to stop the segregationist policies that still pervaded the state of Alabama in the 1960's which I found really interesting.

And they just wouldn't, I mean the Alabama State and the city would just not stop it, at the end of the day.

So that just goes to show that you know, this place here was a bastion of extreme racism. And I wonder from the reaction I got off the shop owner, she turned around and said but oh they disobeyed the law that's why they put the dogs onto the children – and I said, "sorry this was just two blocks down at a shop where I bought food." I had been mortified and intrigued by all this information I had recently learned, and so I told these three women. "Are you serious?" Judy said raising her eyebrows. The other woman muttered and shook their heads. "I am serious" I told them. "Wow," they said in tandem.

"That shows you, you know we have come a long way but there is still a long way to go" Winnie said sadly.

"And her three – her husband and her two sons, are in the police force – current police force" I informed them.

"Oh jeez" Judy exclaimed.

"Well yeah" Sherry said looking around at our faces.

"And that's just walking around, buying food, coming from a local shop" I said.

"We've not come to terms with our history here" Sherry mentioned still shaking her head in disbelief.

"That's one reason why we do the witnesses here," Judy told me matter- of-factly, "to help Birmingham, white Birminghamians, work out what their history means to them. And help them figure out how to orient themselves in regard to the history of their city, which is that, if we are honest, we are in awe of the movement for human rights which took place here, and we can only appreciate and support the great advances in human rights that the courage of black people in Birmingham brought about, and with that reorientation their only response is 'I want to be a part of it, I want to be a part of this movement'. And there are ways for white people to be a part of this movement, and so that's one of our missions is to help people rethink and reorient themselves rather than going around their whole lives with this antagonism and this confusion and this dissociation within themselves and from their city – we want them to feel an integral part of the city, and integral part of this movement, that's why we do it the way we do it."

"Why do you think they are so confused about their history," I asked seriously. And in reply I received their answers.

"Denial" Winnie said. "White people?" I queried.

"That's a philosophical question – fundamentalism, the world over, is going to kill us all, eventually, if anything does," said Judy. "And a lot of it can be laid at the foot of a misguided, exclusionary, punishing religion, that is at the heart and soul of our region – But nothing is exclusively true to the south. If this election has shown anything, it's that the nation is capable of being Alabama."

I felt I had gained a little more insider knowledge, if you would call it that. I thanked them for their time all the same and went on my way.

At the Birmingham Civil Rights Institute, a person showed me an online photo of Michelle and Barack Obama, America's graceful first couple, that had been altered on a computer to make them look monkey- like.

Quite apart from the President himself, I'd always thought Michelle Obama to be America's most elegant first lady since Jacqueline Kennedy. Where did these people who'd doctored the photo get off?

The person who showed me the doctored photo had been crying about it and she was saying "how were these images allowed to be?" And obviously they are allowed to be. I mean where else would you see images like that of the President and his spouse?

This sort of thing would probably be illegal in New Zealand too, not because of the prominence of the people in the image but because it seems that we have somewhat stronger laws against hate speech and incitement than the Americans seem to have. I forwarded the picture to some people in New Zealand, and they were shocked and said I should delete it.

The person who showed me the image told me that her great-grandparents were slaves and she said she has been studying for six years, and she doesn't allow her children to accept what the mainstream media tells them. So, that was very interesting that she said that she doesn't believe anything that she reads in the media anymore, and also that democracy in this country with the Russian hacking is very much in question.

She said she is just going to teach her children what is real. She did think there was a conspiracy or hate campaign against Hillary Clinton, and also blamed the mainstream media for what took place. She thought the media gave Trump the candidate far too much free publicity over all his antics, in ways that eclipsed the fact that the media was mostly critical of him. The images trumped the words.

She's not the only one to have worked that out. Images trump the words, no pun intended. Trump shouldn't have been allowed to hog the TV screens for about eighteen months, as America's number one naughty celebrity.

She just turned around and said that she's going to step back and, you know, watch the show (an apt metaphor). She was very positive about the whole thing, although I gathered that she didn't vote for Trump. She thought he would trip himself up pretty soon. I had to agree, at the end of the day he would trip himself up. It was an interesting conversation.

For more, see:

a-maverick.com/blog/birmingham-alabama-a-much-more-interesting-city

CHAPTER TWENTY-NINE

# *St. Augustine: The oldest city in the USA*

*The St. Augustine waterfront. Pixabay public domain image by Paulbr75.*

I KNEW I was heading all directions and spending a lot of time backtracking ridiculously: but that's okay! I had a list of things to do and places to see and be, and if for whatever reason another one got added to that list – I just went.

That's the fun of it all, I guess. Go where you want and do what you please. A plan, or absence of plan, which was really helped by having an Amtrak railway pass in those places where the trains ran.

There wasn't one from Birmingham to St. Augustine, or not directly at any rate. For this stretch it was about a twelve-hour drive in my rental car from Birmingham, which I felt up to doing. So, I did.

St. Augustine was well worth the trip. Perched on the northern end of the peninsula of Florida, it is a refreshing sea-side town. Founded in 1565 by the Spanish admiral Pedro Menéndez de Avilés. St. Augustine is the oldest continually settled European town on the mainland of the United States of America (Puerto Rico was colonized from 1493 onward).

St. Augustine holds an interesting history behind its paved walkways, blue oceans and intricate colonial inspired buildings. It was once a place of continuous sacking and raiding, either by the English, by Spain or by pirates. Nowadays it is a brilliant and lively seaside town, popular with tourists. So, I decided to do the touristy thing and hop on a bus tour.

St. Augustine has a fair bit of history in relation to the civil rights era as well. As I rode around on the bus, I hoped to learn more about that as well. The St. Augustine Movement began in 1964, with several prominent activists including Martin Luther King Jr arriving in the city to support desegregation of the black community. In June 1964 at the St. Mary Missionaries Church, Dr King spoke to the church members inside.

So many people turned up to hear him speak that they had to hold talks in different churches. Another church they met at was the Trinity United Methodist Church. They were planning a peaceful protest that was going to be held at a motel called the Monson Motor Lodge, on a site now occupied by the Bayfront Hilton Hotel. The protest was organized because, a few days before, they had been refused access to the restaurant at the Lodge.

When they got to the Lodge on 18 June to stage their protest, Dr King's group received further opposition from the manager. Activists of all shades then jumped into a segregated pool at the Lodge, whereupon the owner, Jimmy Brock, tipped in two gallons of muriatic (hydrochloric) acid to generate chlorine fumes and force them out. In a rapid-fire sequence of exposures, Brock is caught in the act by an alert photographer. You can even see the chlorine cloud in one shot. It was all in the newspapers a day or two later.

The notorious Monson Motor Lodge incident, as it is still called today, helped ensure the passage of the Civil Rights Act two weeks later. President Johnson corralled legislators in a room and, pointing to the photographs in some newspaper no doubt, insisted that they pass the Act.

Needless to say, in 1960s St. Augustine it wasn't the deranged motelier but the protesters who were arrested. Dr King himself was held in a cell for one night, a fact that added to the outrage felt by all those who were wondering what on earth was going on in St. Augustine, and down South more generally.

It was great to see the churches and other places where Dr King had held and been part of discussions and actions on civil rights. It is a monumental part of American history, and I was glad I got to see it with my own eyes.

It wasn't safe for Dr King to stay in one place for too long because somebody had placed a bounty on him. He was even asked by the courts to leave St. Augustine for one month because he had, according to them, disrupted the racial harmony in the city.

So, he moved around a lot, even within St. Augustine. He stayed at several homes within the city and each of them now has a specially engraved plaque in front, so they were easy to pick out as we drove around.

It was good to see how the city of Saint Augustine was proud of its civil rights history. Like other cities in the USA, they have since named a street after him: Martin Luther King Avenue. But St. Augustine does have on additional claim to distinction in that it is the only city in the

United States to have a street named after Dr King that he actually marched on.

On the fiftieth anniversary of the Monson incident, the Bayfront Hilton held a benefit luncheon for the public in its restaurant, all ethnicities welcome it goes without saying – a most fitting tribute!

The tour then went to a fort where the bus passengers could get off and have a walk around. The Castillo de San Marcos, completed in 1695, is the oldest masonry fort in the entire United States of America, and it was quite amazing. Shaped almost like a four-pointed star with buildouts from the points of a square, it sits overlooking Matanzas Bay.

Matanzas means 'massacres', and it's a place-name that pops up with disturbing regularity all over the former Spanish colonial empire.

In the case of Florida, the name refers to a Spanish colonial version of the Donner Party incident. With winter setting in (however mild) and with not enough food for the Spanish garrison plus a number of French troops lately captured from an ill-fated French settlement just up the coast in the Jacksonville area, Fort de la Caroline. The French prisoners were massacred by Menéndez's men in order to reduce the burden on the food supply, and that's how the Floridian Matanzas got its name.

Of course, it could be that the Spanish are more honest about the tragic side of life, frontier life included. In New Zealand, we have a bay that used to be called Murderers' Bay or Massacre Bay, which would surely have Matanzas in its name to the present day if we spoke Spanish. But the name was changed to Golden Bay once the more respectable sorts of colonists began populating the area. Where the Spanish are tragic, we are middle-class.

*St. Augustine Sights*

*Top: Aviles Street (oldest street in the USA) and the Bridge of Lions, both public domain images by Paulbr75 via Pixabay. Bottom: Flagler College*

I spent a bit of time wandering around the Castillo before heading back to the bus stop to rejoin the group. They had revolving tours going all the time, so you had the option to get off at some of the locations and spend a bit of time there, just like in Washington.

At any rate, there can't be many cities in the USA that have an honest- to-goodness, fully intact Spanish Castillo right in the middle of town, as if you were in Cuba or someplace like that. In fact, there is only one: and it is St. Augustine.

The next part of my journey was south, to Miami Beach and unknown to me at the time I was in for a very interesting experience.

For more, see:

a-maverick.com/blog/st-augustine-the-oldest-city-in-the-usa

CHAPTER THIRTY

# Miami: Where not all alligators live in the swamp

*Miami waterfront*
*(Pixabay CC0 public domain image by pixiexid)*

MIAMI was my last stop on the mainland of the US, before I headed to the Pacific islands of Hawai'i. I don't know what I was expecting when I arrived. I was aware, as most people are, that Miami was a thriving tourist hotspot. A seaport city with beautiful beaches, lots of partying, and lots of people.

Miami sits in the south of the Florida Peninsula, a nine-hour train journey from St. Augustine via Orlando. Miami is the only major American city founded by a woman, Mrs Julia Tuttle: which is one of the reasons I wanted to visit it.

Mrs Tuttle was a prominent businesswoman and an original landowner in what is now modern-day Miami. She recognised the attractive location and growth prospects of the tip of the Florida peninsula, and lobbied a railway owner of the day, Henry Flagler, to build a railway line into the area. Flagler was skeptical at first, because the far tips of peninsulas normally don't develop very much. Take New York City, for instance: it's at the bottom end of Long Island, not at the far tip, windy Montauk Point, where there isn't much apart from the seagulls. Likewise, most of the development in Michigan is at the south end of the Lower Peninsula, not at the Mackinaw / Upper Peninsula end, even with the bridge.

To add to all that, southern Florida had a reputation for being a pestilential mixture of swamps and jungles, of the sort where explorers stood a good chance of dying of a mosquito-borne fever.

All the same, Mrs Tuttle could see that the tip of Florida and the Keys beyond would one day be a tourist paradise, drawing down visitors from the chilly north, who would seek to get as far south in winter as they possibly could without leaving the US mainland altogether.

Thanks to Mrs Tuttle's persistence, the initially skeptical Flagler eventually did build a railway to the tip of Florida and to the Keys. And so, sprang forth the city of Miami. For a long time, Flagler, the convert to Mrs Tuttle's cause, was commemorated as the 'father of Miami'; until people began to remember, once more, that Julia Tuttle had been its 'mother'.

Miami has been the site of many migrations from Latin America, the Caribbean Islands, and even from Cuba after the Castro Revolution. In fact, about a third of all the people in Miami today would call themselves 'Cuban', even if they were born in Miami.

Anyway, I was staying in a hostel that was about a twenty-minute walk from the seaside areas of South Beach and Ocean View. My first impressions of the hostel, was that it was clean, filled with people from all sorts of countries, and very hospitable. The hostel staff were lovely, really welcoming, and I was excited to be there!

*Miami Waterfront*

*Art Deco buildings and old car, South Beach (Ocean Drive), Miami*
*(Wikimedia Commons image by Massimo Catarinella, 19 June 2008, CC-BY-SA 3.0)*

Walking around South Beach and Ocean View was amazing – the views and surf – I could get why this area was so popular! The first night was cruisy, I didn't meet anybody, and I had dinner by myself. I stayed in a six-bed female dorm. In that dorm, apart from me, were two young women from Argentina in their mid-twenties, a woman from Brazil, and a Venezuelan woman. The staff I came across were all nice and interacted well with the customers.

It was Christmas Eve, and I went down to the beach to lie down on the golden sand and just relax. I met some really nice people down there; everybody was quite friendly. I walked up Ocean Avenue and came across a tasty transvestite fashion show at the Palace Bar. I stayed and watched for two hours: it was a brilliant show! The drag queens and transvestites got up and sung pop, rap, r&b and performed it all so well. They were very classy and danced around together and made jokes – it was a good laugh too! It was the best I ever saw. In New Zealand, I had been to quite a few of these sorts of shows but the ladies in Miami blew them all out of the water!

Back at the hostel one of the staff arranged a tour for me of the Everglades National Park – home of the alligators. The bus driver couldn't tell us about the itinerary, and I had to wait in line for half an hour to show my tickets. The tour took us out on an airboat – something I have always wanted to do – so bucket list check! We had to wear ear plugs because it was so loud, and the driver of the boat was texting, which I thought was hilarious! We skimmed across the water for forty minutes and saw one alligator and a whole lot of birds, but I was thrilled to do it! He told us about all the pythons that had been washed into the national park by a big storm five years earlier, and how they were eating all the baby alligators; and that a lot of people keep them as pets.

The driver took us back to a restaurant where they served alligator! I couldn't eat that: the only thing I could actually eat on the menu was ice cream. The guy who ran it wrestled with an alligator. He was so knowledgeable, and gave a great show.

Alligators look a lot like crocodiles, of course. What's the difference? The main difference is that crocodiles have a special organ that enables them to drink seawater and expel the salt, but alligators don't. So, alligators are confined to habitats where there are plenty of freshwater swamps to maintain a sizeable population. While there are many species of crocodile, only two species of alligators are known to survive today, *Alligator mississippiensis* in the New World and *Alligator sinensis,* the Chinese or Yangtze alligator, in China.

Its swamps transformed into rice paddies, the Chinese alligator is now an endangered species. It is in the same position as Old-World varieties of beavers and bison, and for the same reason. Most people, I'm sure, have no idea that beavers, bison and alligators were once just as common in the Old World as in America, along with the lions that used to roam Europe. But that was long ago, and things are far more domesticated now.

Another difference is that alligators are less aggressive than crocodiles. No doubt, that is why the guy I just mentioned was able to wrestle the alligator without being shredded (a lot of people deplore this sort of exhibition, by the way).

It still pays to be cautious with American alligators, just in case. Though, apparently, the somewhat smaller Chinese alligator almost never attacks anyone and simply strives to keep out of the way of humans instead. Some say, also, that crocodiles and alligators are the fact behind myths of dragons; and that the quietly elusive nature of the Chinese alligator, which has no doubt helped it to survive for thousands of years in a densely populated country where any attack on humans would bring a hue and cry, also explains why Chinese dragons aren't as terrifying as the crocodile-based dragons of other cultures.

As a bad-taste photos I somehow ended up posing for suggests, these days, such wildlife really does have more to fear from us!

*Everglades Tour*

*The Everglades*

So, the beaches and the Everglades marked a great start to my Miami holiday. But it gradually soured the longer I stayed.

On the second day, I did another tour where I made friends with Martha, a 75-year-old woman staying at the hostel. She was holidaying down from New York. She was on quite a good retirement package, and also liked staying in hostels. She met a lot of amazing young travellers from all over the world here – they are from France, they are from Montreal, they are from all around the world. There are even families staying in the hostel, in some of the rooms.

Martha was fantastic and we got on very well. We did coffees out and walks around South Beach.

There are just so many people from all over the world here, holidaying here for a week, getting away from the cold. People are in this hostel – living
here, working here because they, like me, choose to work – they are freelance. I don't get paid for what I write. But people come from the states where there is a lot of snow, down here to work.

275

I shared my room with a woman from Venezuela called Marianela, who worked as a chef for a professional gambler in an upper-class suburb of Miami. On her days off, she would come and stay here, and she stayed at the same hostel one month previously, and she had $400 stolen from her purse – when she went to the shower – by her roommate. She said to her roommate that there was no need to steal the money, I think she told the staff, but nothing was done. So, we were told not to leave our phones out, and to leave nothing out, and to put everything in our locker. So, she was telling everybody here that this hostel had had a high number of burglaries. The two Argentinians got some stuff stolen as well.

Really just a note on South Beach, Miami: come for a holiday and get all your money stolen in hostels. It's the norm, I'm afraid. That's what the police say, and what the owners of the hostels say. I stayed in hostels in lots of other places in the USA, and I have never seen it quite like this.

So, it was a merry Christmas to everyone concerned. The two women from Argentina and their friends all moved into a room together and, after Marienela, I had to share my room with a drunk prostitute and that wasn't much fun.

I went on another boat tour to Bayside with Martha. We saw the homes of Elizabeth Taylor, Rihanna, Jay-Lo and Al Capone, and plenty of artificial islands.

I loved the Bayside food and the saxophone player – what a great location, different from South Beach. Some of the locals have told me that South Beach has definitely improved in the last thirty years – that you can walk through parks, and it is safe most of the time. It must have been really rough before!

On my second to last day, I called the owner of the hostel and spoke to him about the thefts.

The hostel owner said he would do everything to make me happy, and I said all I wanted was for the Argentinians' accommodation to be refunded.

I did meet a lot of very nice people on the beach and in the hostel, even under such unfortunate circumstances.

Lastly, I should add that Miami is threatened by sea level rise, which may already have had something to do with the recent collapse of an apartment building, in the sense that its foundations might have been undermined. As of the time of writing, the final word on that has not yet come out.

For more, see:

> a-maverick.com/blog/miami-where-not-all-alligators-live-in-the-swamp

CHAPTER THIRTY-ONE

# Hawai'i: the world's biggest waves, Hula and Housing issues

Hawai'i

*(Imagery ©2017 Data SIO, NOAA, U.S. Navy, NGA, GEBCO, Data LDEO-Columbia, NSF, NOAA. Map data ©2017 Google.)*

FROM MIAMI, I flew to Kona International Airport in Hawai'i. Hawai'i was meant to be the icing on the cake, my final stop in the USA before heading on home to New Zealand. I had been away for months now and was looking forward to getting back to some normality.

Well, I'll tell you, my introduction to Hawai'i was not the tropical relaxing time that I had envisioned and been looking forward to. I was

279

still in the throes of severe food poisoning picked up in Baracoa, Cuba, a country I visited for three weeks after my stay in Miami: a city to which I then briefly returned in order to catch the plane to Hawai'i. (I write about Cuba in my book *A Maverick Cuban Way*.)

In honour of the fallen astronaut Ellison Onizuka, who grew up locally, Kona International Airport has been officially known since 2017 as Ellison Onizuka Kona International Airport at Keāhole.

Kona International Airport is close to a town called Kailua-Kona on the largest island of the Hawai'ian archipelago: an island that is also known as Hawai'i but more usually just called the Big Island.

From Kona, I caught a local flight to the smaller but more densely populated island of Oahu, more correctly spelt O'ahu, about 250 km or 155 miles to the northwest, where the city of Honolulu and Hawai'is busiest airport by far, Daniel K. Inouye International Airport, are both located. There weren't any direct flights from Miami to Daniel K. Inouye, which is why I arrived at Kona.

Honolulu's famous beachfront suburb of Waikiki was brilliant, but a bit touristy for me!

I got stuck into the food there, I figured it had to be cooked properly! So, I had Mexican corn bread pizza with cottage cheese – delicious! I also got four fajitas for about $10 which I thought was super cheap! While I was sitting there eating I got talking to a young native Hawai'ian guy, and he said he felt his land was invaded. I couldn't help wondering what the Cubans would have done in a situation like that. Well, I suppose the Hawai'ians do have a right to feel invaded. Freedom is priceless.

I also visited a traditional village that had statues so like the Māori ones from New Zealand that I was quite surprised! Though, I shouldn't have been. Māori lore speaks of a semi-mythologised ancient homeland called Hawaiki, cognate with Hawai'i in the same way that I say tomahto and you say tomayto.

*Waikiki*

*(Top image Pixabay CC0 public domain image by Skeeze)*

The New Zealand Māori, Tahitian and Hawai'ian languages are all quite similar, to the point that a Tahitian named Tupaia on Captain Cook's ship Endeavour was able to serve as an interpreter to New Zealand Māori, even though a vast expanse of ocean separated Tahiti from New Zealand.

Since then, there has never been any real doubt that the most immediate ancestors of the New Zealand Māori came from the Hawai'i-to-Tahiti region of the Pacific, 'Eastern Polynesia' as it is known. The ancestral Hawaiki of the Māori is not though to be literally the same as modern-day Hawai'i. But both Māori and modern Hawai'ians have kept the ancient ancestral name in the process of colonizing new lands, one in their folklore and the other in the name they call themselves.

I was booked into a hostel, and really the hostels in Hawai'i are amazing! It only cost me $50 a night to stay in a duplex. Hotels were hideously expensive. I looked online, and by the time you added up all the hidden surcharges and booking fees, hotels were well into the two-to-three hundreds. Over-priced in my opinion – so hostels again it would be.

(A quick note on accommodation arrangements and bookings for future or current travellers, I was using hotels.com, booking.com and hostel world. They have apps for smartphones or tablets, so booking accommodation was actually a breeze! I avoided Priceline though, because they started charging a $50 fee.)

I heard other travellers talking about the Ha'ikū stairway on the island of O'ahu, an incredible climb along 3,922 steps (by one count) along the razor-sharp spine of the Ko'olau mountain range. I don't think I'd make it to them on this trip, but I made a note for next time.

The Haʻikū stairway was originally built by the US Navy in 1942 to facilitate access to a special military radio transmitter called an Alexanderson alternator, a name that just rolls off the tongue.

The Alexanderson alternator produced radio signals at a much lower frequency than ordinary broadcast radio signals. The low-frequency hum of the Alexanderson alternator could be picked up loud and clear all over the Pacific but required huge antennae to intercept it. Ships were large enough to sport the antennae required, and the alternator itself broadcast from an antenna that spanned a whole valley, from mountaintop to mountaintop.

The stairs are nowadays used by tourists hoping to catch sweeping views across the island of Oʻahu. Because of land disputes and liability concerns they are not officially open to the public, and the fine for illegal ascent is $1,000. But daredevils seem to illegally ascend the rickety World War-II- era structure almost every day, regardless: an obviously unsatisfactory state of affairs.

I had prearranged to go back to the Big Island. Roughly 150,000 people live on the Big Island, which is full of stunning scenery and volcanoes. That was my main reason for heading there – volcanoes! My food poisoning was just starting to settle slightly – I still felt off but that was not going to stop me going there. So, I hopped on the plane and went.

I arrived back at Kona International Airport and went straight to the closest Walmart in the nearby town of Kailua-Kona to buy myself a whole lot of camping gear, as it was my plan to go and camp all around the island. I had read up my guidebook, and it suggested going camping because it was a great way to see everything on an island that wasn't too overrun by tourists, apparently. The campsites around

Hawai'i are mostly located out of the towns and are a better way to see the real Hawai'i.

It turned out that camping in Hawai'i is an effort, a big effort with a lot of thinking ahead and planning involved. My guidebook told me to just turn up and pitch my tent – in fact, you have to book online. I turned up at one campground in Kohanaiki Beach Park near Kailua-Kona and just pitched my tent. I stayed there for one night, and then I had to move on because I hadn't pre-booked, and I didn't have a permit.

Well, it was lucky for me then that I ran into a guy called Dana from San Diego, who was staying on a campsite at another locality called Spencer Beach Park. He said he'd lend me his permit to use while I was there until I could sort something out. So, I stayed for two nights with him at the Spencer Beach Park. We talked and enjoyed the scenery and life in general.

He was an interesting character. He had been homeless in the mainland of the United States but had wound up here after a rather eventful and sad journey. He had lived in San Diego and there was a set up for homeless people there by the state government where they gave land to the homeless where they could build themselves homes or whatever they needed. Quite a grand gesture too. Anyway, Dana had set himself up quite well – built himself a house and a room he rented out on Airbnb to earn some extra cash. The thing though is that in areas like that you don't always get the loveliest of people – so it ended up the neighbours were dodgy and running a methamphetamine lab, right next door.

I do believe that some people just seem to miss out on things in life through no fault of their own. Sometimes it's just down to bad luck and getting taken advantage of by other people. Sometimes people can even be too trusting. He told me how a book he had sent to the publishers was stolen and published by someone else. (He has since written six books, and good on him.)

Anyway, it was quite interesting just sitting there and listening to his take on life and his stories. He left San Diego after living there for seven years. As he told it, the meth lab neighbours worked with some crooked police officers and Dana ended up having his house burnt down, and all his stuff stolen, and then the neighbours accused him of threatening them with a gun, so he ended up in jail for 5 weeks. It turned out they were lying and so he got off the charge. One of the neighbours who had accused him was in court because she had a list of criminal charges herself – I'll bet one of them was stealing his stuff.

I don't judge homeless people – I know that sometimes it is simply bad circumstances that lead them to where they are.

I got a rental car and drove down the coast past Kailua-Kona and Kealakekua Bay, the site where Captain Cook was killed in 1779. I loved the scenery – it was beautiful and reminded me a little bit of home in New Zealand. I also went for a short stroll in one of the national parks there, I wanted to do more walking and trails – but that wasn't going to happen!

I heard about a local Hula festival that would be happening at the Sheraton hotel that night, so I decided I would go. It was well worth doing and the Iolani Luahine Hula Festival held so much meaning behind it. Iolani Luahine was a well-known Hula dancer, famed in Hawai'i for her dancing. She enrolled at one of the missionary schools set up on the island, only to find out Hula dancing was forbidden, so she changed schools. After graduating from university, she started up Hula classes – realising her goal in life was to keep the traditional dancing alive. She made huge steps in preserving the cultural dancing and so the festival is in memory of her and her efforts. I was so glad I went. It was fascinating to watch the performance and a really good show.

I met a lot of people on the beach who were homeless. They would put up a hammock every night and would sleep there on the beach. I talked to a few of them. Homelessness affects our societies, and something needs to be done. One lady I met was in her fifties and she did studies for the council – she smoked cigarettes and marijuana and then couldn't afford housing, so that's how she wound up homeless. I ended up sharing half my breakfast with her and getting her a coffee while she talked to me about her situation. I think I had enough after a few days though, it does get tiring – you can't help everyone, and you can't give 24/7. Anyway, a lot of the locals told me that they felt Hawai'i had become a dumping ground for the mainland USA homeless, which was quite sad.

I also heard about the now ex-CEO of Facebook, Mark Zuckerberg, and how he had been trying to file a lawsuit to force the sale of 'quiet titles' to the land surrounding his home that he brought with wife Priscilla Chan in Hawai'i. Land rights in Hawai'i were of interest to me. Hawai'ians traditionally use a system like many other Pacific Island countries whereby ownership of land is passed through the family without formal deeds of transfer, only oral tradition, which can result in people having title to bits of land that they don't even know about, if the traditions start to be forgotten.

Zuckerberg claimed that for most of the owners he identified, after careful research, the compensation that he planned to pay would have been a welcome and unexpected windfall. However, the whole thing looked a bit suspect to many people all the same, part of a long process of alienation of native Hawai'ians from their own land. A sugarcane magnate named Spreckles was one of the first 'Californian white' people to obtain land in Maui – purchasing vast amounts of it from the King. His sugar cane farm became one of the largest in the world.

Traditionally Hawai'ian people believe land is 'aina' – a spiritual entity that cannot be owned! Anyway, at the end of January 2017, Zuckerberg and Chan said that they would only buy land from willing sellers and would give up trying to force people to sell land that they weren't doing anything with right now.

Hawai'i was the 50th State to join the United States, and with a population of 1.4 million people, it is the only US state that lies in Oceania or Polynesia. Sadly, of the 1.4 million people who call Hawai'i home only 30,000 of them speak the language as native speakers although this is up from as few as 2,000 in the late 1990s. It must be undergoing a revival in the schools and preschools, much as Māori did in New Zealand some thirty or so years ago.

My next stop was in Kalapana. I made my way there feeling horrible and almost delirious from my bug and went to one of the first beach resort hostels I saw – I got a room for $60 a night, I think they felt sorry for me in my dire state. But it was great and the lady, Anita, who ran it was lovely. (One Hawai'i travel tip – ask the locals where to stay. You might get cheaper accommodation that way!)

I stayed there for two days trying to recover – I think it was just the constant travelling that was wearing me down also. On the first day, I ate some packaged tuna – not canned stuff – with gluten free pasta and tomatoes and that set me off again. I was getting really fed up so on that third day I pumped myself full of pills and made a spur of the moment booking. I thought, to heck with this cheap lifestyle, I am going on a helicopter ride – so I did. It wasn't cheap but I was getting sick of feeling sick – ha!

*Helicopter
Ride over
Volcano
Field*

So, off I went. What an experience! For a better view, there were no doors. They were worried about things blowing out into the rotor blades. So, they told me to make sure everything I had was thoroughly secured.

It wasn't till we had taken off and I'm looking down and my jandal (or thong) clad feet that I regretted not wearing my sneakers, which I had literally worn for the last four months except today. I spent the whole time worrying either that I was going to vomit or that my jandals would blow off into the rotor blades and that would be the end of that.

It was an amazing flight, one I thoroughly enjoyed and would do again.

(Yes, I got a flutter in my stomach: not because of the food poisoning but because I can get scared of heights!)

You could bike from Kalapana to go and look up close at the eruptions and the lava. I found this place called 'Uncle Robert's' and that's where I got talking to a lot of the locals. The locals I talked to were sick of the homelessness. Homeless people stole their food and were living in public buildings in Pahoa and then accidentally burning them down, buildings like the Akebono Theatre. Fair enough, too, that they were sick of that.

One thing I noticed around the island was the abundance of wild fruit that just grew everywhere. Avocados in particular were everywhere and all over the roads!

I went up the coast to Hilo and did a very silly thing. I brought this sausage meat that should have been heated up more, it was merely warm. So, I ate it along with some vegetables and boom, hello, return of food poisoning.

Apart from that, Hilo seemed to be a quaint and pleasant town.

I flew back to O'ahu once more, for I was to depart for New Zealand from Daniel K. Inouye International Airport. Also, I wanted to visit O'ahu's North Shore to see the Banzai Pipeline: the huge wave system that is ridden in the world-famous local surfing competitions. And yes, Hawai'i is where surfing was invented – when the first European explorers arrived it was already an established tradition. O'ahu's North Shore was a great place to finish off my trip although I am still annoyed that I couldn't eat any of the beautiful island food.

For more, see:

a-maverick.com/blog/hawai-i-the-worlds-biggest-waves-hula-and-housing-issues

CHAPTER THIRTY-TWO

# *Homeward Bound*

O N the way back to New Zealand, I had time to reflect on my incredible experiences of the USA. Already things were going from bad to weirder with Trump.

What will become of the great United States in years to come? Will it rediscover its mojo to become a true leader of what we used to call the free world, or will it dwindle into the sort of place that's seen better days? Will the Federal Government in Washington become increasingly irrelevant as its prestige declines and as conflicts with states and cities intensify?

One thing I have seen in my travels is that the USA is a huge and diverse country. This we know already, but I have proven it to myself all over again. The cities, at one time the weakest tier of government in America, are increasingly assertive, and increasingly where the action is. Maybe in the long run the USA cannot hold together except in the loosest of ways, and if that leads to more democracy and civics at the local level, it may not be a bad thing.

I would never have envisaged that the USA, which has fomented so many coups in other lands, would suffer its own attempted coup on January 6, 2021. I could not believe the polarization of the population, division and hatred and related crimes, the seeming disintegration of an empire and the refusal of the Republicans to allow an inquiry into the events of that day

The Black Lives Matter Protests have also become necessary. Trump's growing ban from mainstream media, Twitter and Facebook, and Biden's calm, may allow for a healing of the wounds inflected by Covid and the previous administration.

# *Thank You*

*First and foremost, I'd like to thank all the wonderful people I met while I was travelling through the United States, because without them I wouldn't have been able to write my book.*

*Thank you for giving me an insight into your lives and allowing me the time to talk to you all. Thanks to all the people I met on the train who kept me going with our interesting conversations.*

*I'd like to thank my friends in Detroit who were kind enough to take me around, William J. (Bill) Chandler and Diane West (now Gorsky). A massive thanks to Bill for writing the history chapter for this book.*

*Thank you to my friend Aubray in Wichita Falls, for showing me around and taking me to one of the last drive-through liquor stores! Thank you to people I met in Little Rock and allowing me to join in on your Democratic election party.*

*Thanks to long-time Red Hook residents Ellie Spielberg and Russell Bittner.*

*Lastly, thanks to my editor Chris Harris for all his hard work in getting this book and its associated blog posts together.*

*As always, all errors or omissions that may remain are mine.*

# Other books by Mary Jane Walker

Did you like *A Kiwi on the Amtrak Tracks?* If so, please leave a review!

And you may also like to have a look at the other books I've written, all of which have sales links on my website a-maverick.com.

## A Maverick Traveller

A funny, interesting compilation of Mary Jane's adventures. Starting from her beginnings in travel it follows her through a life filled with exploration of cultures, mountains, histories and more.

## A Maverick New Zealand Way

The forerunner of the present book, *A Maverick New Zealand Way* was a finalist in Travel at the International Book Awards, 2018.

## A Maverick Cuban Way

Trek with Mary Jane to Fidel's revolutionary hideout in the Sierra Maestra. See where the world nearly ended and the Bay of Pigs and have coffee looking at the American Guantánamo Base, all the while doing a salsa to the Buena Vista Social Club.

## A Maverick Pilgrim Way

Pilgrim trails are not just for the religious! Follow the winding ancient roads of pilgrims across the continent of Europe and the Mediterranean.

## A Maverick USA Way

Mary Jane took Amtrak trains around America and visited Glacier, Yellowstone, Grand Teton, Rocky Mountain and Yosemite National Parks before the snow hit. She loved Detroit which is going back to being a park, and Galveston and Birmingham, Alabama.

## A Maverick Himalayan Way

Mary Jane walked for ninety days and nights throughout the Himalayan region and Nepal, a part of the world loaded with adventures and discoveries of culture, the people, their religions and the beautiful landscapes.

## A Maverick Inuit Way and the Vikings

Mary Jane's adventures in the Arctic take her dog sledding in Greenland, exploring glaciers and icebergs in Iceland, and meeting some interesting locals.

## Iran: Make Love not War

Iran is not what you think. It's diverse, culturally rich, and women have more freedoms than you would imagine.

## The Scottish Isles: Shetlands, Orkneys and Hebrides (Part 1)

In 2018, Mary Jane decided to tour the islands that lie off the coast of Scotland. She made it around the Orkney and Shetland groups, and to the inner-Hebrides islands of Raasay, Mull, Iona and Staffa as well. She was amazed to discover that Norse influences were as strong as Gaelic ones, indeed stronger on the Orkneys and Shetlands.

## Catchy Cyprus: Once was the Island of Love

This is a short book based on Mary Jane's visit to Cyprus, the island that copper's named after and the legendary birthplace of Aphrodite, Greek goddess of love. A former British possession in the Mediterranean Sea, Cyprus is divided into Greek-dominated and Turkish-dominated regions with United Nations troops in between.

## Lovely Lebanon: A Little Country with a Big History

"I visit the small country of Lebanon, north of Israel, a country whose name means 'the white' in Arabic because of its snow-capped mountains. Lebanon is divided between Christian and Muslim communities and has a history of civil war and invasion. For all that, it is very historic, with lots of character packed into a small space."

## *Eternal Egypt: My Encounter with an Ancient Land*

In this book, Mary Jane explores Egypt, a cradle of civilisation described by the ancient Greek historian Herodotus as the 'gift of the Nile'. Mary Jane put off going to Egypt for years before she finally went. She's glad she did: there's so much more to Egypt than the pyramids!

## *The Neglected North Island: New Zealand's other half*

In this book Mary Jane explores New Zealand's less touristy North Island. *The Neglected North Island* was judged **'Best Antipodean Cultural Travel Book 2021'** by *Lux Life* magazine (lux-review.com) and is also a **2021 IPPY Awards Bronze medallist** in Australia/New Zealand/Pacific Rim – Best Regional Non-Fiction

## *The Sensational South Island: New Zealand's Mountain Land*

In this book, which is the companion to *The Neglected North Island,* Mary Jane explores New Zealand's mountainous South Island. She branches out from obvious tourist traps like Queenstown to explore this large but thinly populated island's lesser-known byways, historic cities and diverse landscapes, which vary from subtropical jungles where the world's southernmost palm trees grow, to much chillier places that look like Iceland and Greenland and even like Mars.

## A Nomad in Nepal

*A Nomad in Nepal and the Lands Next Door* updates Mary Jane's earlier book, *A Maverick Himalayan Way*. With links to blog posts containing colour photographs and videos, *A Nomad in Nepal and the Lands Next Door* describes Mary Jane's three trips, so far, to Nepal and the Himalayan region.

Delving deeply into Himalayan history, *A Nomad in Nepal* is also a mine of useful firsthand experience about guiding and trekking pitfalls and the politics of the region, all while describing epic treks in Nepal and visits to Sikkim, Dharamshala (Himachal Pradesh), Sringagar (Kashmir) and the exotic Chitral region of Pakistan as well, hard-up against Afghanistan, where the local Kalash tribe is menaced by the Taliban.

Made in the USA
Coppell, TX
23 November 2021

66281317R00180